The nave and west towers of Aberdeen Cathedral

MEDIEVAL ABBEYS AND
CATHEDRALS OF SCOTLAND
Mike Salter

FOLLY PUBLICATIONS

ACKNOWLEDGMENTS

The plans were all drawn by the author and are largely based on material obtained during his many field trips in Scotland between 1977 and 2010. Most of the plans are at 1:800 scale but those of the cathedrals of Brechin, Dunblane, Kirkwall and Lismore, the priories of Beauly, Brough of Birsay, Monymusk, Restenneth, and Strathfillan, the abbeys of Fearn and Inchcolm, Iona nunnery, and the friaries of Elgin, Luffness, Peebles and St Andrews are all at the larger scale of 1:400. The map is also by the author.

Thanks are due to Peter Ryder for pictures of Ardchattan Priory, Cambuskenneth Abbey and the friary at Inverness. Thanks to Sarah Miles for pictures of the abbeys of Crossraguel, Holyrood, Inchcolm, and Sweetheart, and that of Oronsay Priory. All other photos were either taken by the author (the majority are recent digital pictures taken 2006 - 2010) or are old pictures in the author's collection, eg the postcard of Dornoch Cathedral. Thanks are also due to Max Barfield, who drove on the expedition across Mull when Iona was visited by the author, and to Jenny Harper, who drove when Peebles, Kilwinning and Lesmahagow were visited. Thanks also to Paul and Allan at Aspect Design for help with the cover design and other artwork matters.

AUTHOR'S NOTES

The aim of this book is to present information and comparative plans of the remains Scotland's cathedrals, abbeys, priories and friaries dating between the early 12th century and the 1560s. For information on Early Christian monastic sites such as St Blane's on Bute which did not become either cathedrals or monasteries later on, and also the fine series of later medieval collegiate churches in Scotland, see the companion volume Medieval Churches of Scotland (which replaces the author's 1994 publication The Old Parish Churches of Scotland). Lack of space has prohibited much discussion of the post-monastic history of the sites, or descriptions of modern furnishings, stained glass and monuments in those buildings remaining at least partly in use.

There is a deliberate imbalance in the amount of material given about the sites in favour of lesser known ruins, so that Oronsay Priory is given almost as much space here as Arbroath Abbey, and the cathedrals of Dornoch and Fortrose are given nearly as much space as the far more magnificent and complete cathedral of Glasgow. This is because places such as Arbroath and Glasgow have guide books and have been adequately described previously in many other publications. Most of Scotland's fifty friaries are also very little known and again this book attempts to redress the balance.

ABOUT THE AUTHOR

Mike Salter is 57 and has been a professional writer and publisher since he went on the Government Enterprise Allowance Scheme for unemployed people in 1988. He is particularly interested in the planning and layout of medieval buildings and has a huge collection of plans of churches and castles he has measured during tours (mostly by bicycle, motorcycle or on foot) throughout all parts of the British Isles since 1968. Wolverhampton born and bred, Mike now lives in an old cottage beside the Malvern Hills. His other interests include walking, maps, railways, board games, all kinds of morris dancing, mumming, playing percussion instruments and calling folk dances.

Dunfermline Abbey

CONTENTS

A map of the sites appears inside the front cover

GENERAL INTRODUCTION

Very little is known for certain of the origins of Christianity in Scotland and there is much uncertainty as to how it developed and was organised prior to the 11th century. The monastery at Whithorn is said to have been founded by St Ninian as early as c400 but the main stimulus to the growth of Christianity in Scotland seems to have been the founding of the Irish Celtic monastery on Iona by St Columba in 563. The Celtic monasteries did not adopt the code or Rule of St Benedict written c529, which, with modifications and changes of emphasis by the different orders, became the basis of all monastic life in mainland Europe throughout the medieval period. In fact the Celtic church remained quite isolated from developments in Europe. Each of its centres seems to have been quite independent of each other and of any outside control, although there is little evidence that this led to laxity as might be expected. The priests were allowed to marry and abbacies sometimes became hereditary.

The Celtic church trained and sent out missionaries but failed to establish and maintain a proper system of parochial churches tended by local priests overseen by a bishop who assumed spiritual authority over an area known as a diocese. The word cathedral was used to describe a principal church in a diocese in which a bishop had his seat or throne, known as a cathedra. Having discarded bishops in favour of abbots an eventual decline of the Celtic church in the face of competition by the highly organised Roman church was inevitable, although some of the major monasteries of Culdee or Celtic priest-monks survived into at least the 13th century. Centres of the Celtic church in places which had only parish churches rather than monasteries or cathedrals in the medieval period, such as St Blane's Church on Bute, lie outside the scope of this book but are described in the companion volume Medieval Churches of Scotland.

England had many large Benedictine abbeys established during the Saxon period and an even larger number of small priories established by the Normans after they arrived there in the late 11th century. Ordinary unreformed Benedictine monks arrived late in Scotland from England and were never numerous. In the 1070s Malcolm III's spouse Margaret, an English princess of the Saxon line introduced them at Dunfermline and in the 12th and 13th centuries they appeared also at Coldingham and Iona. Most of the Scotland's nunneries were originally Benedictine but some appear to have affiliated to the Cistercians later on. The earliest order of reformed Benedictines adhering to a stricter interpretation of the Rule were the Cluniacs, who had just two major houses in Scotland, at Crossraguel and Paisley, plus a small cell on the Isle of May.

Another order of reformed Benedictines, the Tironensians, noted for encouraging craftsmen to join them, were favoured by 12th century Scottish kings, possibly as a way of being different to England, where the order never had a single house (although there was one in SW Wales). The establishment of monasteries was a way of extending royal influence and providing centres of culture and learning in remote areas. Monasteries also had guest houses which could be used as comfortable places for transient kings and nobles to stay in. Alexander I established the Tironensians at Selkirk but during the long reign of his brother David I, when much was done to reorganise the Scottish church, this community moved to Kelso to be close to the major royal castle at Roxburgh. David also settled Tironensians at Lesmahagow, William the Lion established a second major royal Tironensan abbey at Arbroath, and William's son David founded the abbey at Lindores. The order also had a fifth major abbey at Kilwinning, and a small priory at Fyvie. Yet another order of reformed Benedictines without representation in England or Wales were the Valliscaullians. In the early 13th century three priories were founded for them in Scotland, at Ardchattan, Beauly and Pluscarden.

Remains of a monastery at Brough of Birsay unrecorded in history

The most numerous order of monks in Scotland were the Cistercians, who arrived from Rievaulx in Yorkshire to Melrose in 1136 and Dundrennan in 1142. Other houses soon followed at Coupar Angus, Glenluce, Kinloss, Newbattle and Saddell, and more were founded in the 13th century at Balmerino, Culross, Deer and Sweetheart. There were houses of Cistercian nuns at Berwick, Coldstream, Elcho, Haddington, North Berwick, Manuel, and St Bathans. The order rather reluctantly accepted nuns later on and some of these houses were originally Benedictine. Whereas the Benedictines had an emphasis on liturgy, which in wealthy Cluniac houses became extremely elaborate and complicated, the Cistercians favoured simplicity, remoteness and self-sufficiency. Their churches never formed part of the parochial system. The Cistercians liked remote valleys where their lay brethren (who spent considerably less time in church than the choir-monks) could tame wilderness and turn formerly harsh environments into highly organised and eventually profitable farms raising crops and huge flocks of sheep.

The most austere of all the medieval monastic orders were the Carthusians. They became popular in the later medieval period when the houses of other orders had to some degree become lax in their ways partly as a result of external influences resulting from their need to farm and trade. The Carthusians only Scottish house was an early 15th century royal foundation at Perth. Their houses normally only had a dozen hermit-like monks, each had his own house and garden in which he stayed most of the time, services in church being less frequent, and communal eating even less so.

Carthusian houses and friaries ranked as priories with a prior as their head and most nunneries were also priories ruled by a prioress. Larger establishments of the other orders, and all Cistercian houses regardless of size, ranked as abbeys under the rule of an abbot, with a prior as his deputy and often a sub-prior as third in command. There was no fixed rule as to whether a house should be an abbey or priory. In England the priors of Cluniac houses usually presided over establishments bigger than many of the abbeys of other orders. Priories were normally under the control of a mother house, often in another country. Scotland's remoteness made this a less practical arrangement, and more of its monastic houses ranked as abbeys. Most monasteries eventually held considerable estates which required a considerable amount of administering. Their heads were often away either supervising the estates, on pilgrimage or official business to Rome, or in attendance on other religious rulers or secular courts.

In addition to the various orders of monks there were two orders of canons regular, so called to distinguish them from the lay clergy that served most of Scotland's cathedrals. Regular canons also lived a cloistered life as part of a community, sleeping in dormitories and eating in refectories and adhering to the basic monastic vows of poverty, chastity and obedience. However they also went out into the wider community to preach and take services in the parish churches under their control. The western part or nave of their own abbey or priory church usually served the needs of a parish. First introduced by Alexander I at Scone, the Augustinians or black canons had more houses than any other order in Scotland. At Inchaffray, Iona, Monymusk, Restenneth and St Andrews they were seen as the natural successors to Culdee priests. The cathedral priory at St Andrews and the royal abbeys of Cambuskenneth, Holyrood, Jedburgh and Scone were large and well-endowed establishments. There were more modest houses of Augustinians at Blantyre, Canonbie, Inchcolm, Inchmahome, Oronsay, Pittenweem, Restenneth, and still more minor priories at Monymusk, St Serf's, St Mary's and Strathfillan, whilst there were Augustinian nunneries at Iona and Perth. These communities followed a rule put together in the 11th century which was based on the writings of St Augustine of Hippo in the early 5th century. The more rather austere Premonstratensians or white canons also used the rule of St Augustine. They arrived at Dryburgh in 1152, and later established other houses at Soulseat and Tongland in Galloway and Fearn up in Ross. The priests at Whithorn also adopted the Premonstratensian rule.

There were also two military orders of knights who lived as monks. The Knights Templar had commanderies at Temple in Lothian and Maryculter in Grampian plus a number of other holdings which were manors where revenue was raised rather than actual monasteries. Accused of all manner of nefarious practices on account of their wealth and secrecy, the Templars were suppressed in the early 14th century and most of their possessions in Scotland passed to the Knights Hospitaller, whose Scottish commandery was at Torphichen. The Hospitallers used the Rule of St Augustine. The numbers of knights in these orders in Scotland would have been few, and most of the inhabitants at the commanderies would have been servants and lay officials.

The nave at Holyrood Abbey

Doorway from church to cloister at Dryburgh Abbey

Transept doorway at Kirkwall Cathedral

South side of the church at Arbroath Abbey

The south aisle of Fortrose Cathedral

During the first half of the 12th century Alexander I and his younger brother David I established most of Scotland's mainland sees and at the same time the lord of Galloway re-established Whithorn as a bishopric. Scotland eventually had twelve sees but Orkney was originally a Norse see subject to an archbishop at Trondheim until 1472. The see of Argyll centred on Lismore was only divided off from Dunkeld in the early 13th century. A bishopric of the Isles nominally centred on Iona was a still later creation, the Isles having been originally subject to a bishop on the Isle of Man. Despite David I's efforts to have one created there were no archbishops in Scotland until St Andrews was made an archdiocese in 1472, and that of Glasgow was made another in 1492. The archbishops of York claimed jurisdiction over the Scottish mainland until the late 12th century when the Pope recognised the independence of the Scottish Church, and exempted all the sees there except that of Whithorn from jurisdiction from York. Glasgow was by far the largest Scottish see, extending into the western and middle march areas of the border with England, whilst the see of St Andrews included Berwickshire, the Lothians, Fife and also parts of Angus and Kincardine, thus reducing the tiny see of Brechin to mostly scattered parishes. Aberdeen and Elgin were also large and wealthy sees. Large western parts of the poorer sees of Caithness, Dunblane, Dunkeld, and Ross were mountainous waste. In the early 13th century the cathedral of Caithness was moved further south to Dornoch, that of Ross moved slightly from Rosemarkie to Fortrose, and that of Moray from Spynie to Elgin, having originally been at Birnie.

The cathedrals at St Andrews and Whithorn were served by regular canons but the other cathedrals were served by secular canons, each supported financially by a prebend usually consisting of one or more parishes. Each canon would have his own house run by servants close to the cathedral and would appoint a vicar to conduct services within the parish supporting him which might be some distance from the cathedral. It was quite normal for canons to be frequently absent on business in their parishes or serving in the constantly moving retinues of kings, lords and bishops since they were amongst the very few educated men at that time. Thus the prebendaries often also had to provide and clothe a priest to take their place in the daily services in the cathedral, these priests being known as vicars choral. Even a small and poorly endowed cathedral like Brechin had as many as 14 prebendaries and that at Glasgow eventually had as many as thirty two. The prebendiaries formed a body known as a chapter, usually independent of the bishop and led by four officers known as the dignitaries, who consisting of the dean (the administrative head), the precentor (in charge of music), the chancellor (the businessman of the chapter) and the treasurer.

East end of the presbytery at St Andrews Cathedral

The last remaining pier of the Dominican friary at Inverness

In addition to the dozens of communities of monks, regular canons and nuns in Scotland there were also fifty houses of the various orders of friars. These establishments have been largely overlooked until fairly recently because very little remains of any of them and historical information about them is also often scanty and obscure. The first friars to arrive were the Trinitarians, who were established at Aberdeen and Berwick before King William the Lion died in 1214. Later in the 13th century other houses were established at Dunbar, Failford, Houston. Those at Dirleton and Peebles were founded in the 15th century and perhaps also those at St Andrews and Scotlandwell. The Trinitarians sometimes took over existing hospitals or churches, as at Peebles. Their houses usually had endowments from estates and tithes and dues of churches that they served in order to enable them to fulfil their original aims of local charitable works and paying the ransoms of crusaders held captive by foreign powers.

The other orders of friars were mendicants (beggars) and were not supposed to hold property apart from the land on which their house, cemetary, gardens and water supply were located. Sometimes the communities even had to pay rents on parts of these and it was generally accepted that friars continually had to beg for alms as well as preach. Thus mendicant friars usually had to rely on the continued generosity of local benefactors both for building works and everyday subsistance. Consequently friars' houses were generally within towns large enough to be able to support such communities of beggars. The friars provided a supply of extra preachers and their teaching encouraged the establishment of universities. They were often well supported by royalty and local bishops, although as competitors for local charity they were generally unpopular with the established communities of monks and regular canons and also with the local parochial clergy. Mendicant Franciscan and Dominican friars first appeared in Berwick, Edinburgh, Elgin and Perth in the 1230s and soon spread to other towns, whilst the Carmelites first settled at Perth in the 1260s. The Augustinian friars and the Crutched friars each only had a single Scottish house at Berwick-on-Tweed (then a part of Scotland) but the Carmelites eventually had ten houses, the Dominicans fourteen houses, and the Franciscans sixteen houses, including several later houses of Observants.

Many of the friaries were later medieval foundations, such as the Carmelite houses in Edinburgh, Linlithgow and South Queensferry, the Dominicans at St Monans (who took over an older church) and the Franciscan houses in Aberdeen, Edinburgh, Glasgow, Jedburgh, Kirkcudbright, Perth and Stirling. Some of these later houses were for the much stricter Observant Franciscans. The town of Berwick-on-Tweed had as many as six friaries by the end of the 13th century and was then clearly a much more important place than it is today. Aberdeen was prosperous enough to have had four friaries by the end of the medieval period, Edinburgh and Perth each had three and Ayr, Dunbar, Elgin, Glasgow, St Andrews and Stirling each had two. Single houses of mendicant friars lay at Banff, Dumfries, Dundee, Haddington, Inchbervie, Inverkeithing, Inverness, Jedburgh, Kirkcudbright, Lanark, Linlithgow, Luffness, Montrose, Queensferry and Wigtown.

A large monastery could have quite a number of officials under the abbot and prior. Church services were organised and managed by the precentor, who was the chief singer and also the librarian and archivist. He might have an assistant known as the succentor, The sacrist looked after the fabric of the church and its ornaments, vestments and furnishings, usually having an office beside or near the east end of the church. His deputy the sub-sacrist rang the bells to summon the brethren to services. The cellarer was in charge of supplies of food and drink, often extending to dominion over the mills, brew-house and agricultural work at the abbey's possessions, although these might be looked after by a lay steward, whilst the sub-cellarer or kitchener had responsibility for the preparation and cooking of food. The fraterer was in charge of serving the food and drink and the cleaning of the refectory and the lavatory outside it where the monks washed their hands before eating. A chamberlain was in charge of providing bedding, hot water for shaving and occasional baths, and the provision of clothing for the brethren. Novice monks usually used some of the lower rooms in the east range and were under the supervision of the novice master. Sick and elderly monks went to an infirmary separate from the main buildings (usually further east). It was looked after by the infirmarer and was normally the only place where meat other than fish was served. Monks regularly went there to be bled (which was thought to be good for the health) and were allowed to eat meat to help recover afterwards. Most monasteries had some sort of guest house and that required another official to administer it. In the larger monasteries guest houses were mansions of some size suitable for visitors of high rank with their retinues. The guest houses at Dunfermline and Holyrood were frequently used by royalty and were developed as royal palaces long before the Reformation. Idle conversation was discouraged by monastic rules but of course officials would have needed to have spoken frequently to each other and to other monks and servants under their control.

The rule of St Benedict allowed for a daily monastic routine with up to seven services, with some variance according to the season of the year and certain feast days requiring special services, extra masses or processions. Some of the office holders must have been excused from attending some of the services at certain times in order to carry out their duties. In some communities menial tasks such as cooking and washing were done by servants. The day started with Matins in the middle of the night, which was quickly followed by Lauds. Then the monks were allowed the second part of their sleep for about four hours before returning to church for the service of Prime. Some reading time, then the all-important masses for the souls of benefactors and their families and then some refreshment followed, then the Lady Mass. Afterwards the monks gathered in the chapter house to hear read a portion of the rule under which they lived. Weekly duties were then allocated, faults were corrected and any business conducted relating to such matters as administration of estates, construction or repair of buildings, appointment of officers or the admission of novices. The next service, Tierce or High Mass might be followed by a procession around the church and cloister. The monks then took their main meal of the day in the refectory. A good choice of foodstuffs would usually be on offer. Originally meat was served only to sick and elderly monks in the infirmary but later on meat eating was normal. Monks were not allowed to indulge in idle chat during meals and were obliged to listen to one of their number reading religious tracts from a pulpit in the refectory. Afternoons were used for study, writing, the teaching of novices, short periods of recreation, or just a nap during the longer days of summer. A second meal was taken after Vespers or Evensong and after Compline the monks would retire to bed for three hours or so for the first part of their sleep until wakened again for Matins.

The east end of Dunkeld Cathedral

Old print of the former arcade at Dornoch Cathedral

By the late medieval period many of the monasteries were not in a healthy state. Numbers of monks, canons and friars were down, standards had become lax in some houses, and those communities within reach of English raids had at least some buildings that required re-roofing or other substantial repairs. One or two, such as the nunneries at Berwick-on-Tweed and Lincluden, had earlier ceased to be viable communities and had already been suppressed. Normally religious communities held free elections to appoint their own heads and other officials, but this had always been subject to occasional interference by the secular or religious authorities because the heads of large monasteries had influence and power that made them great temporal lords. For instance, a number of them were entitled to a seat in parliament. From the 1490s onwards there was a tendency in Scotland for a lay commendator to be appointed to look after an abbey's estates and external affairs instead of an abbot. Frequently the commendators were younger sons of the royal family or the family regarded as being descendants of the founder and thus entitled to burial rights within the abbey church. Some of the commendators were able administrators, and did enough to keep the buildings in repair and services maintained, but others (some of them even under the age of majority) saw monastic estates purely as a form of private revenue.

Not many Scottish monasteries were actually officially suppressed, i.e. closed on a specific day. The Reformation Parliament of 1560 did away with catholicism in Scotland but monks were often allowed to remain in situ until they died out for lack of recruits as long as they accepted the changes brought about by the Reformation or were very discrete about continuing with services that could be considered as Catholic in form. Many of the friaries were already closed by 1560 since mendicant friars could no longer collect enough alms to support themselves in Scottish towns. Friars and regular canons either became Protestant clergymen or fled abroad. Except at Elgin, Fortrose, and St Andrews, where only fragments have survived, the cathedrals also served as parish churches and remained in use as such. At Aberdeen, Brechin and Whithorn only the nave was needed for that purpose, and at Dunblane, Dunkeld and Lismore only the choir remained in use, whilst at Dornoch the nave eventually lost both its aisles. At Glasgow and Kirkwall the buildings were subdivided to allow simultaneous use by multiple congregations and the whole survived to be re-unified in more modern times. The nave at Dunkeld and the choir at Brechin have been restored in more recent times.

Sedilia in the choir of Inchmahome Priory

Refectory and precinct gateway at Dunfermline Abbey

Sweetheart Abbey

By the 1590s most monks in Scotland had died out and their possessions eventually became hereditary in the families of the lay commendators, many of whom got former abbey lands officially erected into baronies by James VI in the early 17th century. Sometimes, as at Ardchattan, Newbattle, Balmerino and Glenluce, parts of the claustral buildings became the mansions of these families, although the last two were later abandoned. At Arbroath the abbot's house continued to be used. At Dunfermline and Holyrood the former guest ranges had already begun to be adapted as royal palaces well before the Reformation.

Where monastic churches served parishes parts of them remained in use as with the choir Coldingham and the naves at Dunfermline, Pittenweem, Holyrood and Whithorn, although the latter two have since become ruinous. Part of a small nunnery church at Abbey St Bathans also remained in use. The east part of the church at Culross was taken over for parochial use, although it did not originally serve such a purpose and at Elgin a roofless but otherwise fairly complete Franciscan friary church has been re-roofed to form a school chapel. Two thirds of a former Carmelite church at South Queensferry now forms an Episcopal church. The guest range of the Franciscan friary at Inverkeithing still remains roofed and parts of two other friaries in Aberdeen remained in use as a college and hospice until the mid 19th century. The majority of monastic buildings became ruinous and were eventually plundered for their materials. This happened very quickly in towns, where the sites of former friaries were valuable and soon redeveloped, hence the lack of remains of most of them. Excavations have revealed small parts of two in Aberdeen and most of the main buildings of the Carmelite house at Linlithgow, whilst footings still remain of the church at Luffness and a ruined transept at St Andrews. There are also some standing remains of the Trinitarian friaries at Dunbar and Peebles.

During the 20th century Pluscarden has been re-occupied and partly restored by Benedictine monks and another religious community has taken over and restored all the buildings at Iona. A high proportion of the remains of Scottish monastic buildings have been in state care now for several generations. Historic Scotland now maintain Glasgow Cathedral, ruined parts of cathedrals at Dunkeld, Elgin, Fortrose, and Whithorn, plus what remains of the monastic buildings at Arbroath, Ardchattan, Beauly, Brough of Birsay, Cambuskenneth, Deer, Dryburgh, Dundrennan, Inchcolm, Inchmahome, Iona, Jedburgh, Kelso, Melrose, Peebles, Restenneth, Saddell, St Andrews, Sweetheart, and Torphichen.

The meagre remains of the church of Saddell Abbey

South side of the ruined church at Beauly Priory

The church and east range at Pluscarden

ARCHITECTURAL INTRODUCTION

Very little remains of the Celtic monasteries in Scotland. Their churches seem to have been simple in form, consisting of a nave for the congregation and a shorter, narrower and lower chancel to contain the altar and its attendant priests. Early towers remain at Restenneth and Brechin, the latter being round like the numerous series in Ireland. Square towers at Dunblane and St Andrews also pre-date the existing cathedrals.

Of the new wave of 12th century churches on more ambitious plans the earliest structures of any size now remaining are the nave at Dunfermline and the transepts and choir at Kirkwall, both probably of the 1140s. Nothing remains of the original east end at Dunfermline but both buildings are smaller versions of what had recently been completed c1130 at Durham. Each had an aisled nave originally intended to have two western towers, transepts with eastern chapels and a central tower, an aisled choir and a presbytery extending further east, which at Kirkwall was originally apsed. All the openings were round-arched, with splendid doorways of many orders with nook-shafts and pilaster buttresses clasping the external corners and along the sides. The main arcades had large round piers, those at Dunfermline decorated with motifs such as chevrons, and having octagonal cushion capitals. Above was a triforium gallery and then an upper storey of windows known as a clerestorey. Over the aisles were ribbed vaults, a common feature in large churches of all periods. The choir at Jedburgh also of the 1140s has a design in which the triforium appears to be slotted into the upper part of the main arcade arches, a design also found at Romsey in southern England.

Inside the nave of Dunfermline Abbey

St Andrews has only minor fragments remaining of a large cathedral of this type, begun in the 1160s and eventually modified to take a high vault over the presbytery. There the transepts were so long that there was space for each one to have three eastern chapels beyond the aisles of the choir. A cruciform layout with a central tower as at Dunfermline, Jedburgh, Kirkwall and St Andrews was the norm for abbey churches and cathedrals across Europe by the 12th century. However transepts were absent at the smaller and poorly endowed Scottish cathedrals of Dunblane, Dunkeld, Fortrose, and Lismore, and nothing of former transepts now survives at Brechin or at Whithorn. The latter was the only one of this group of cathedrals to have a central tower. At Glasgow the transepts were an afterthought and do not project beyond the outer walls of the aisles.

Dunblane has a tall mid 12th century tower left over from an older layout awkwardly abutting the south side. Restenneth has a still older tower set within the south side and Lismore has footings of a former tower at the west end of the nave. The cathedrals of Brechin and Dunkeld each have a later medieval NW tower lying north of the nave west end, and there are remains of other towers in this position at the priory of Inchmahome, and the abbeys of Lindores and Cambuskenneth, the latter a detached structure still complete. Most cruciform buildings were intended to have central towers but they were sometimes never actually raised above roof levels. Towers were originally officially banned in Cistercian churches, although there are later examples of them at Sweetheart and Melrose still standing. Pairs of western towers were sometimes a feature of cathedral and abbey churches. The 13th century examples at Arbroath and Elgin and the 15th century pair at Aberdeen take the place of the westernmost bays of the aisles, which is the normal layout, whilst Holyrood has one surviving tower of a 13th century pair set beyond the outer corners of the aisles. The church at Kelso was unique in Scotland in having a second western transept with another central tower. The square bay to the west of it seems to have functioned as a grandiose porch.

The larger churches usually had a lean-to roofed aisle on each side of the nave. In Scotland the only cathedrals with aisled choirs were at Elgin, Glasgow, St Andrews and Whithorn. Elgin had the distinction of outer aisles forming chapels on both sides of the nave. Iona and Whithorn were unusual in that they once had aisled choirs but the naves never had aisles. The very modest cathedral at Lismore was aisleless, and that at Fortrose only gained a south aisle to contain tombs later on. Modest priories like Archchattan and Beauly and poorly endowed abbeys like Saddell usually had cruciform churches with aisleless naves. The church at the Templar preceptory at Maryculter was just a plain oblong and this form was also common for friary churches, as at Elgin, Linlithgow and Luffness, whilst the friary at South Queensferry had also a low central tower and a south transept. The monastic churches at Balmerino, Cambuskenneth, Deer, Inchmahome and Lindores, plus the nunnery church at Iona, only had a single aisle, always located on the opposite side of the nave from the cloister.

North doorway at Arbroath Abbey   *Fragmentary western towers at Arbroath Abbey*

Remains of the west doorway at Kelso   *Arch from south transept to a chapel at Kilwinning Abbey*

Cistercian churches tended to have just a short presbytery east of the crossing, and the monks' choir stalls often lay within the eastern part of the nave, whilst the rest of the nave was allocated for use by the laybrothers. Otherwise naves in abbey churches were often used by parishioners. Another feature of Cistercian churches was the suppression or minimisation of the triforium gallery, which was basically decorative rather than functional. Sweetheart is a late example of this. The Premonstratensians had the same aims and their church at Dryburgh originally had a minimal triforium, small openings only being introduced at that level later on.

It often took several generations to complete the construction of a cathedral or abbey church. Usually work started at the east end of the church and progressed westwards as far as the crossing. Then, as at Glasgow, Kirkwall and Jedburgh, there would be a lull whilst more materials and funds were accumulated before work could be resumed to complete the nave. By then the east end was often considered too small or old fashioned and needed to be remodelled or entirely rebuilt. Often, as at Holyrood, work on a larger new aisled building would begin around a still remaining smaller structure, and, by the time the latter was demolished and materials had been accumulated to resume the work, a change from the late Romanesque style with round arches to the early Gothic style with pointed arches had been decided upon. Evidence of such work of c1180-1220 and the gradual adoption of the pointed arch especially used in blind arcading can be seen in the churches at Arbroath, Coldingham, Dryburgh, Dundrennan, Holyrood, Kelso, Kilwinning, Jedburgh, and St Andrews. Of these the works at Coldingham, Holyrood and Jedburgh are the most complete. Holyrood was the only one of these originally designed to have a high vault and has fine foliage capitals on the columns of the blind arcading. The nave at Kelso was rather unusually built layer by layer, instead of bay by bay, the top level being fifty years or so later than the bottom level.

The cathedral at Glasgow is essentially a 13th century building although representing three separate campaigns of work. The whole east end has two storeys, allowing pilgrims to circulate around both the shrine and the tomb of St Mungo. The work is characterised by tall lancet windows and buttresses of greater projection than in the 12th century. Almost all of the cathedral at Elgin was also built in the last three quarters of the 13th century. Most of what eventually stood at Brechin, Dornoch and Dunblane was also of that period, although the first two have seen much 19th century rebuilding. The priories of Beauly and Pluscarden also have good 13th century work in their churches. What remains of the church at Culross straddles the change from the 13th to the 14th century. At Dunkeld the choir was rebuilt in the 14th century and the nave in the 15th century. The south aisle of the nave was the only part designed for vaulting and the piers are simple plain cylinders, a type last used in the 12th century. Most of the surviving work at Aberdeen, Crossraguel, Melrose and Paisley is also late medieval, the work at Melrose being necessitated by destruction wrought by an English raid in 1385. Aberdeen gained two new west towers with machicolated parapets with a row of lancets between them for a west window. Crossraguel lost its transepts in the rebuilding. Paisley is a rare Scottish abbey church still completely roofed (Iona is the other), but all the upper walls of the choir and the transept gables are modern rebuilding. Most of the new church built at Inchcolm in the 15th century is now reduced to footings apart from one wall of the south transept with stub remnants of a pointed barrel-vault.

A SE view of Brechin Cathedral

The twin west towers of Aberdeen Cathedral

15th century window at Torphichen

Late 13th century multiple lancet window at Inchmahome

15th century window at Glenluce

A development from the single lancet windows at Coldingham and Restenneth was to group lancets together as in the east window at Inchmahome. Piercing the spandrels between the heads of grouped lancets created plate tracery, first seen in the triforium at Jedburgh of c1200-10 and then developed c1240-60 in the choir at Glasgow and the nave at Dunblane, and still further developed in the transepts of the 1270s at Glasgow. The east end at Elgin continues the tradition of tiered lancets seen earlier at St Andrews and Arbroath but the presbytery at Sweetheart probably of c1280-95 has windows of two, three and five lights with Geometrical tracery. Other, more restored, examples of this can be seen at Glasgow. Warfare stalled most building projects in Scotland during the early 14th century. The church begun at Fearn in the 1340s reverted to old-fashioned simple lancet windows. The protracted rebuilding at Melrose gives us firstly interesting examples of rectilinear tracery of c1400 combined with panelling and image niches in buttresses inspired by contemporary work in England, and then 15th century aisle windows with flowing tracery, a style by then outmoded in England but still in fashion elsewhere in northern Europe. Similar windows appear at Paisley and in the collegiate church at Lincluden and there were once others in the choir at Crossraguel. Loop tracery of c1520 appears in the transept of the Dominican church at St Andrews and in some of the collegiate and parish churches (see Medieval Churches of Scotland).

West range of Pittenweem Priory, later used as a manse

The church of Melrose Abbey from the south.

The meagre remains of the church of Cambuskenneth Abbey viewed from the tower top.

Usually the cloister was located on the south side of an abbey church where it would catch the sun, but for drainage reasons the cloister and its buildings lay on the north side of the churches at the abbeys of Balmerino, Iona, and Melrose, plus the Franciscan friary at Jedburgh. None of the Scottish cathedrals served by secular canons had cloisters. Cloister alleys were usually lean-to roofed and had unglazed open arcades towards a central garth. Those at Inchcolm and Inchmahome had alleys set within the structure of the lower storey of the surrounding ranges, a layout more common in remote parts of Ireland. The cloister alleys were used for reading and cupboards for books often remain just to the east of the doorway into the church at the NE corner.

The east range normally contained the dormitory with a latrine or reredorter at or near the south end. The day stair from the dormitory usually lay near the cloister southeast corner, but there was normally also a night stair direct from the dormitory into the adjacent transept (see photo of the south transept at Pluscarden on page 119). The many rooms below the dormitory would usually include a sacristy next to the church, then perhaps a passage connecting the cloister and a cemetery to the east between the sacristy and the chapter house, which often projected beyond the range east wall. Lower rooms beyond the chapter house seem to have been used for such purposes as training novices, but might also include a warming house with a fireplace.

The range opposite the church contained the refectory and sometimes a kitchen as well. Usually there would be a lavatorium for hand washing in or just off the cloister alley adjacent to the refectory entrance. This might be anything from a modest recess in the cloister alley wall to a separate structure projecting into the cloister garth. In the larger Cistercian houses the refectory was set north to south with just one end of it touching the cloister alley and the west range contained the refectory and dormitory of the lay brothers. In houses of other orders west ranges were used to contain stores or guest rooms or provide accommodation for the abbot or prior. The most complete sets of claustral buildings in Scotland are at St Andrews, Crossraguel, Dryburgh, Inchcolm, Iona, and Oronsay, whilst fairly complete single ranges remain at Ardchattan, Inchmahome, Paisley and Pluscarden. Elsewhere only footings or low walls mostly survive.

Ruins of the church of the nunnery on Iona

Chapter houses often survived ruination of the other parts because they could be used as meeting rooms or mausoleums, or happened to lie in a range later adapted as a mansion. Vaulted ceilings, sometimes with internal piers, were common. The room usually had a bench round the walls and canopied stalls for the dignitaries. In large monastic houses it often had an entrance doorway flanked on each side by a two-light window, as at Dryburgh, Dundrennan, Kilwinning and St Andrews. Inchcolm has a 13th century octagonal chapter house and there was once another at Holyrood. Dryburgh has a good late 12th century chapter house and later medieval examples remain at Crossraguel and Glenluce. Amongst the cathedrals Elgin has a fine octagonal chapter house (with a late medieval vault using a central pier), whilst narrow rectangular ones remain at Dunkeld and Fortrose, all of these being located on the north side of the eastern arm. Glasgow has a square two storey 13th century chapter house unusually located at the NE corner of the cathedral.

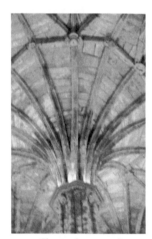

Chapter house vault at Elgin Cathedral

Originally the head of a monastery was supposed to sleep in a dormitory with the other monks but they became great lords and were either frequently away or kept busy conducting the business affairs of the house. By the 13th century the heads of monasteries normally had their own suites of rooms. That at Arbroath is still fairly complete, although most of its features are late medieval. Other buildings away from the main claustral group might include a separate guest house, an infirmary, and a bakehouse. Other buildings such as barns, workshops and stables mostly used by servants might lie further away nearer to the gatehouse to the precinct. A modest gatehouse is the only remnant of the abbey at Cupar Angus. There are more substantial gatehouses and precinct walls at Arbroath, Crossraguel and St Andrews, the latter with an extensive and almost complete late medieval precinct wall adorned with turrets and crenellations.

In the south wall of the eastern part of a church there would commonly be elaborate stone seats called sedilia for priests and these are a common survival (see page 11) as at Crossraguel, Dundrennan, Dunkeld, Inchmahome, Lismore and Paisley. Next to each altar would be a piscina for draining and washing out vessels used during a mass and these also are common. Stone screens or pulpitums remain at Glasgow and Inchcolm. These are the only furnishings which usually survived the ravages of reformers. Most of the stained glass windows, fonts, pulpits, screens and altars bore brightly painted images of saints and other icons which reformers associated with catholicism. Consequently hardly any of them survived the ravages of the 1560s. Dunkeld has some late medieval stalls, and a few battered medieval floor tiles survive here and there.

Originally the abbeys and cathedrals contained the majoirty of Scotland's medieval tombs with effigies since most of the ordinary parish churches were too small and humble to contain them. The mid 13th century knight at Dornoch, a late 13th century knight at Luffness, two bishops and a couple of the 13th century at Dunblane, a bishop at Elgin and a couple of c1300 at Inchmahome are the earliest of the thirty-odd fully three-dimensional effigies still remaining, probably less than a twelfth of the number that must have accumulated in these churches by 1560. Some of the cathedrals may have contained up to twenty or more monuments with effigies and even the churches of humble friaries and small priories must have had at least one or two. Over half of the surviving effigies are of bishops and abbots and the remainder are mostly of men in armour, three with wives. The only example of a man in civilian custume earlier than the post-reformation period is at Aberdeen. There are also a few small odd fragments such as those of a bishop in the site museum at St Andrews. The effigies were often painted, so that the shields of arms bore their real-life colours. Indents of brasses from the 14th century onwards also remain in several churches, with a good example at Iona, whilst Dunkeld has a similar incised slab showing a priest. Inchmahome, Oronsay and Saddell have grave covers with a variety of motifs, including swords, ships and figures of armed men shown in half-relief, this being the normal type of monument out in the western seaboard. Tomb recesses often survive without effigies, and there are other monuments such as that of the Countess of Ross set between arcade piers at Fortrose, where no effigy has survived.

FURTHER READING

Pulpitum screen at Glasgow

Ecclesiastical Achitecture of Scotland 3 vols,
    David McGibbon & Thomas Ross, 1897
Medieval Religious Houses In Scotland,
    I.B.Cowan & D.E.Easson, 1976
Medieval Scotland, Peter Yeoman, 1995
Scottish Abbeys and Priories, Richard Fawcett, 1985
Scottish Medieval Churches, Stewart Cruden, 1986
Three Scottish Carmelite Friaries, Judith Stones, 1989
See also the volumes of the Buildings of Scotland series
and also Inventories of Ancient Monuments by R.C.A.H.M.S.
Guide pamphets in some form exist for: Aberdeen, Arbroath, Beauly, Crossraguel, Deer, Dryburgh, Dunblane, Dundrennan, Dunkeld, Elgin, Glasgow, Holyrood, Inchcolm, Iona, Kelso, Kirkwall, Jedburgh, Melrose, Paisley, Pluscarden, Restenneth, St Andrews, Sweetheart, Torphichen & Whithorn

GAZETTEER OF ABBEYS, PRIORIES AND CATHEDRALS

ABBEY ST BATHANS Borders

Cistercian Nuns NT 759623 20km SE of Dunbar

Much of the small existing parish church dates from 1867-8, but the east wall with a small mid 13th century window with plate-tracery is a relic of a church that in medieval times served both the parish and a small Cistercian nunnery. The cloister and its buildings seem to have been on the north side, where a blocked doorway still remains. Traces of foundations suggest they extended further east than the church. An effigy of a 15th century prioress lies in a modern niche in the church east wall

Abbey St Bathans Church

ABERDEEN FRIARY Aberdeenshire *Carmelite* NJ 941061 S side of the city

Much of the site of the Carmelite friary founded c1270 on reclaimed land by the harbour is built over. Excavations in the 1990s found footings of the west range of the cloister 24m long by 7m wide containing four rooms including a kitchen with a fireplace and a drain. A coin in the foundations dated it to the 15th century. The angle-buttressed NW corner of the late 13th century nave of the 35m long church was also uncovered with a north doorway close to it, along with over two hundred burials from the early 14th century onwards just in the west part of the church. The friary must have been adversely affected by the adjacent battle in 1336.

ABERDEEN FRIARY Aberdeenshire *Dominican* NJ 939064 North side of city

Schoolhill, Black Friars Street, St Andrews Street and Harriet Street surround the site of a Dominican friary of St John the Baptist destroyed in 1560, although much of the precinct wall stood until at least 1661. Slight traces of the old buildings were discovered when the site was cleared in the 1833 for construction of Robert Gordon College.

ABERDEEN FRIARY Aberdeenshire *Franciscan* NJ 942064 NE side of city

A college founded by George Keith, 5th Earl Marischal in 1593 stands on the site of a Franciscan friary founded in the 1460s. Parts of the 15th and 16th century buildings survived in use until the site was cleared in 1835 for the construction of grand new buildings of granite now used as city council offices. Excavations in 2009 found the skeletons of seven men assumed to be friars beside footings of the north wall of the church. The college chapel lies on the site of the eastern part of the church, but nothing earlier than a door dated 1674 now remains.

ABERDEEN FRIARY Aberdeenshire *Trinitarian* NJ 942060 South of the city

King William and Queen Ermengarde are said to have established the Trinitarians here near the junction of Guild Street and Trinity Street c1211. The friary had a church dedicated to the Holy Trinity and is first mentioned in 1273. Many records of minor benefactions to the friary still survive. More major benefactors from at least the 1490s were the Menzies family, one of whom, Gilbert, took possession of the buildings after the friary was suppressed in the 1560s. The former friary was sold in 1631, shortly after a new minister was appointed by Charles I, but the medieval church and modified domestic buildings continued to function as a hospice of some sort with an original gateway until the site was cleared in the 1840s and 50s.

ABERDEEN CATHEDRAL   *Secular Canons*   NJ 939088   2km N of city centre

It appears to have been in the 1130s that the main church of the northeasterly diocese of Scotland was transferred from Mortlach to what is now called Old Aberdeen, a separate centre somewhat to the north of the present city centre. Construction of a new cathedral dedicated to St Machar must have been well advanced by the late 1150s, when the Pope authorised Bishop Edward to provide it with a chapter of monks or canons. Just one abacus from the capital of a pier now remains of it. By the mid 13th century new bishops were elected by a chapter composed of the four principal officers of Dean, Precentor, Chancellor and Treasurer, plus seven ordinary canons supported by prebends and an Archdeacon. Soon after his appointment in 1282 Bishop Henry Cheyne began work on a larger new choir to accommodate this chapter, which by the late medieval period numbered as many as thirty priests. Just one capital from one of the window rere-arches now remain of this choir. Robert I ordered it to be completed at the bishop's expense after peace finally came again to Scotland in the 1320s.

What remains of the transepts and the two large compound western piers of the former central tower seem to represent a new campaign of work commenced by Bishop Alexander Kinninmund in the 1350s. It appears that the foundations of the existing aisled nave were also laid at that time, although the granite superstructure was only completed in the 1420s and 30s under Bishop Henry Lichton. Then, as now, it was used for parochial services. The south side has a buttressed porch and mostly three-light windows but the northern windows are of just two lights. At the west end there is a central doorway surmounted by seven round-arched lancets of equal height. Each aisle is terminated by an angle-buttressed tower with a machicolated parapet surround-

-ing a top stage surmounted by a stone spire divided into three stages by crenellated banding, these spires being added in the 1520s by Bishop Gavin Dunbar. The towers were obviously a 15th century modification to the original mid 14th century design and resulted in the seven bays of cylindrical piers being set out of line with the outer buttresses. This meant that the stone vaulting originally envisaged was never provided over the aisles, although Bshop Ingram Lindsay is said to have covered the nave itself with stone slabs in the 1440s and 50s. It currently has a fine heraldic ceiling of the 1520s added by Bishop Dunbar. It bears 48 shhields of Pope Leo X, the Holy Roman Emperor, St Margaret, the kings and princes of Christemdom and the bishops and earls of Scotland. The clerestorey windows over the arcades are round-headed single lights of very modest size.

Tomb of Bishop Dunbar at Aberdeen Cathedral

During the 1460s and 70s Bishop Thomas Spens glazed the windows of the western parts and provided a new episcopal throne, altar and stalls in the choir. In 1511, towards the end of his episcopacy, Bishop William Elphinstone began work on a timber-framed belfry and spire on the central tower and he also covered the other roofs with lead sheets. Bishop Elphinstone also began work on yet another new choir which was of four bays with a polygonal east apse and had a square sacristy on the north side. Despite providing the spires of the towers and the new roof of the nave, plus a remodelling of the south transept to form his burial place, Bishop Dunbar seems to have left the new choir incomplete, since the high altar was still placed against the east arch of the crossing when it was destroyed by reformers in 1642. His successor, William Stewart adapted the west end of the north aisle as a consistory house and provided the fine pulpit with renaissance detail now transferred to the chapel of nearby King's College founded by Bishop Elphinstone. The choir was demolished in 1560 and the transepts have been ruined since the central tower collapsed in a storm in 1688. See photos on pages 1 and 19.

Surviving monuments include effigies of Walter Idill (a 15th century town official), and a canon shown in an almuce. There are other monuments to Simon Dodds (an official under Bishop Elphinstone), and the 17th century Bishop Scoughall.

The nave of Aberdeen Cathedral

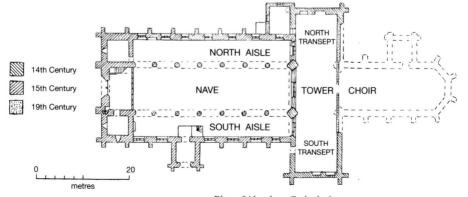

14th Century

15th Century

19th Century

NORTH TRANSEPT

NORTH AISLE

NAVE

TOWER   CHOIR

SOUTH AISLE

SOUTH TRANSEPT

0   20

metres

Plan of Aberdeen Cathedral

ARBROATH ABBEY Angus *Tironensian*   NO 644414   On the east side of town

In 1214 King William the Lion was buried by the high altar of the abbey dedicated to St Thomas Beckett which he had founded in 1178 for monks brought over from Kelso. The abbey became the richest in Scotland, with a mitred abbot and a church nearly 90m long. Not much is known about the early abbots except that Robert, eighth abbot was expelled by his monks in 1267. Henry, thirteenth abbot, was also unpopular but managed to stay in office with support from King John Balliol. Here in 1320 a royal chancery clerk serving under Abbot Bernard de Linton, who was King Robert's secretary and chaplain, drew up the Declaration of Independence, a letter to Pope John XXII in which the Scottish people denied the claims to supremacy of the Kings of England. Commendators were appointed instead of abbots from 1503, the second being George Hepburn, killed at Flodden in 1513. Three of the Beaton family successively served in this role, each eventually becoming an archbishop either at Glasgow or St Andrews. The office later became hereditary in the Hamilton family. The abbey was officially dissolved in 1560, when three of the 22 monks became ministers of the reformed Church. The other monks were allowed to remain in the abbey until they died out.

South transept at Arbroath Abbey   *Gatehouse at Arbroath Abbey*

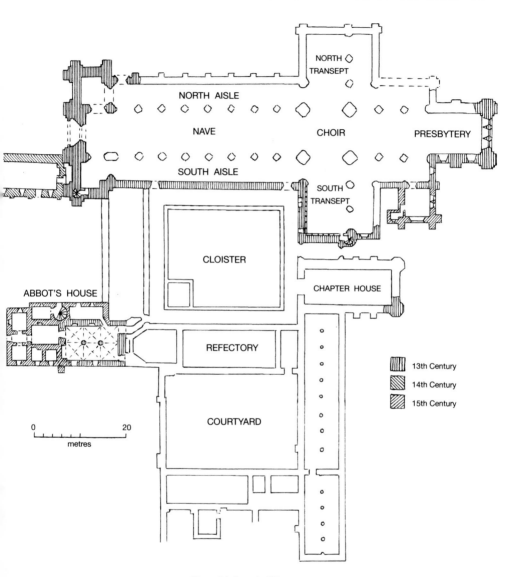

Plan of Arbroath Abbey

Most of the main buildings at Arbroath are thought to have been nearly completed by 1233, in which year the church was dedicated. Its design seems to have been inspired by recent work at Hexham. The aisled nave, now only represented by its south aisle wall and a few pier stumps, extended for eight bays east of a fine pair of heavily buttressed west towers with wall-arcading and a doorway between them set in a deep barrel-vaulted recess over which was a galilee chapel and passages. The towers were not divided internally into separate storeys by floors but the arcades treat them as though they were, with a ninth arch opening into them. The fine north doorway for laymen lies just east of the NW tower. The east end with one surviving tier of three lancets over blind arcading remains of a four bay presbytery flanked by two bay chapels extending beyond a vanished central tower with transepts with eastern chapels. The south transept still stands high with three tiers of blind-arcading with both round and pointed arches on single and clustered shafts, wall-galleries, tall lancets and a large circular window (rebuilt 1809) in the gable, where it could actually light the roof-space. Projecting south from the chapel on the south side of the presbytery is a vaulted sacristy in one corner of which is a raised treasury chamber only accessibly by a ladder. The sacristy was added by Abbot Walter Paniter (1411-49) whose worn arms appear over one of the aumbries. In 1517 the church contained as many as 12 side altars.

The cloister was rectangular, being longer from west to east. The abbot's rooms now mostly of c1500 set upon an older vaulted cellar beyond the kitchen at the southwest corner still stand complete to serve as a museum in which now lies King William's headless effigy. Post-reformation use as a manse and then as a factory and later on a school ensured the survival of this building, albeit in a rather altered condition. Little remains of the other cloister buildings, apart from footings of the reredorter at the south end of the nine bay long east range and a fragment of the chapter house SE corner, plus parts of a range on the south side of a domestic courtyard to the south of the refectory. Extending west from the SE tower of the nave is a guest house range of c1300 with a vaulted basement, beyond which is the main monastic gateway with its vaulted four bay long passage once closed with a portcullis. Beyond the gateway extends the buttressed wall (originally with a range behind it) of the precinct wall out to a square corner tower of considerable height with corbels for a machicolated parapet dominating the High Street of the burgh. See pages 7 & 17.

Ardchattan Priory

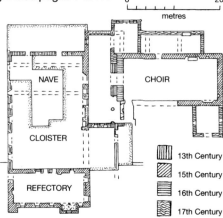

Plan of Ardchattan Priory

ARDCHATTAN PRIORY   Argyll   *Valliscaulian*   NM 971349   6km E of Connel

Duncan MacDougall, Lord of Lorn, established a small priory of Valliscaulians dedicated to St John the Baptist beside the north shore of Loch Etive c1230. Here in 1309 Robert Bruce is said to have held a parliament of the western chiefs. As laid out over twenty years or so after it was founded the priory had a small cloister about 15m east-west by 16m north-south with a refectory to the south, a chapter house and dormitory to the east, and the nave and narrow aisle of the church to the north. There were transepts each with two eastern chapels and probably a central tower. The parts freely accessible to the public are the transepts with a 16th century arch opening into the large new 15th century choir about twice the size of the modest original 13th century one. The gardens of a house later developed from the refectory are also sometimes open.

In the late medieval period a new church had been built to the NW to serve parishioners who previously must have used the nave of the priory church, but this must have been abandoned by the 1620s and is now much ruined. At some point after the priory was suppressed in the late 16th century the choir and transepts were taken over for use as a parish church again, remaining in use until a new church was completed in 1732, after which they were robbed for their materials.

The walls of the priory church are best preserved where burial enclosures of 1614 and 1620 adjoin the eastern end of the choir south side and the middle of the choir north wall. The latter aisle lies on the site of a sacristy reached through a surviving 15th century doorway. Further east the north wall contains a tomb chest recess backed against where the aisle of 1620 was extended eastwards in 1713. There is also a lower recess on the south side. The south wall of the wide new 15th century choir blocked the east window of the northern of the south transept chapels. The doorway from the crossing towards the former nave and the west window of the north transept are 15th century, when there was considerable rebuilding around those parts.

The original refectory range was mostly rebuilt in the 15th century and has some roof trusses remaining from that period. In c1610-20 the former commendator, Alexander Campbell, converted it into his residence. By the late 19th century it was known as Ardchattan House and had a new wing to the west, whilst the main block had been doubled in width by extending north over much of the space of the former cloister, with wings either side of a small court extending into the space of the former nave. Outbuildings further north incorporate part of the north wall of the aisle. Since 1713 the east part of the refectory has been divided off by a new crosswall to create what is now known as the Prior's Room. Here the 15th century south wall has a projection containing two tiny vaulted bays, one was once the refectory pulpit and the other contained steps up to it. Restored in 1960, the bays are divided by a pier formed of a cluster of filleted columns.

AYR FRIARY   Ayrshire   *Dominican*   NS 340219   On the north side of town

Black Friars Walk near the river (off the High Street) and in the vicinity of the old tower of St John's parish church commemorates the Dominican friary of St Catherine founded here in the 1230s by Alexander II and a local burgess named William Malvoisin. Few records of either of Ayr's friaries have survived.

AYR FRIARY   Ayrshire   *Franciscan*   NS 339220   On the north side of town

The Franciscan friary founded in the 15th century lay just upstream from the Auld Brig on the south side of the River Ayr.

BALMERINO ABBEY   Fife *Cistercian*   NO 357247   4km SSW of Tay Bridge

In 1225 the widowed Queen Ermengarde began to acquire land for establishing an abbey for Cistercian monks. A party of them arrived from Melrose in 1229. Her son Alexander II granted a founder's charter to the abbey in 1231, and by 1233 the choir was sufficiently advanced for Ermengarde's body to be buried in front of the high altar. The abbey was burned during the Earl of Hertford's invasion of 1547, and its church was plundered by reformers in 1559. John Hay became the lay commendator in 1561 and later remodelled the east range of the cloister buildings north of the church into a house. The monastic lands were made into a temporal barony in 1605 for Sir James Elphinstone, who took the title Lord Balmerino.

Low walls and buried footings excavated in 1896 remain of the 66m long church of St Mary and St Edward, with a three bay long presbytery lying east of a central tower with transepts each having two eastern chapels. Only the SW corner and the base of one pier of the seven bay arcade remain of a south aisle added to the nave, perhaps around the time of when the monks were given a quarry at Nydie in 1286. The arcade piers were oddly out of line with the shafts dividing the bays of the nave north wall. The north transept retains a west doorway to the site of the cloister and a north doorway towards a sacristy. This room was adapted as the kitchen of the late 16th century house, with a new circular staircase turret added west of it. The original rib-vaulted chapter house beyond later became a vestibule to a new square chapter house added in the 15th century with square-headed windows. The day stair to the dormitory from the cloister lies in the wall between the tunnel-vaulted parlour to the north and the vestibule, being later altered to ascend direct from the latter. Beyond the parlour are two vaulted cells, one of them lying over another cell entered from the west. Over these cells lay the reredorter, with its drain on the east side. This indicates a comparatively short dormitory about 20m long suggesting there were never more than twenty monks. To the NE lies one vaulted room of the lower storey of the 15th century abbot's house.

The original chapter house at Balmerino Abbey, later a vestibule to the new one

The east range at Balmerino Abbey

BANFF FRIARY   Aberdeenshire   *Carmelite*   NJ 692639   On east side of town

Excavations in 1985 prior to construction of a new supermarket in Carmelite Street found sherds of medieval pottery but no actual traces of structures of the former Carmelite friary, which was founded in 1324 by King Robert I, who had a castle here.

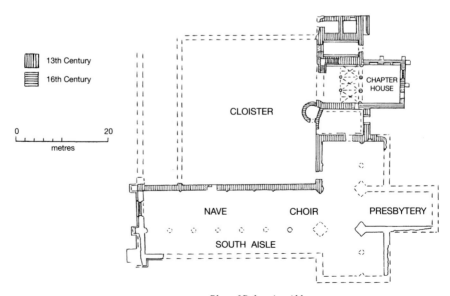

Plan of Balmerino Abbey

BEAULY PRIORY   Highland   *Valliscaulian*   NH 528465   At NE end of village

This priory of for Valliscaulian monks from Burgundy was founded in 1230 by Sir John Bisset of the Aird, whose castle of Lovat lay across the river not far to the east. There were still a prior and four monks here as late as 1571, although by then the lands were under the administration of Walter Reid as commendator or lay prior. The cloister and its buildings are said to have been demolished to provide materials for the new Cromwellian fort built at Inverness in the 1650s but the 13th century church still survives fairly complete since it was still in use in the Cromwellian period. The aisleless nave was remodelled by Robert Reid, prior from 1530 to 1558 (also Abbot of Kinloss and Bishop of Orkney). His arms lie in a niche set under the central one of a group of three west lancets, below which is a doorway with a hoodmould with its stops resting on the Five Wounds of Christ on one side and the sacred IHS monogram on the other.

On the south side the nave windows were set high up above the lean-to roof of the north alley of the cloister. The easternmost windows were spherical triangles with cusped trefoils, and fine rere-arches. There are of a type not common in Britain, but also found at Pluscarden Priory and in Westminster Abbey. Just stubs remain of the walls of the west range. On the north side a doorway led through to the chapel of the Holy Cross added c1416-40 by Hugh Fraser of Lovat and now otherwise only represented by its piscina in the SE corner. The nave also has a piscina in the south wall, where there was an altar set against a screen closing off the monks' choir which was additionally lighted by a pair of two-light windows facing north. There are further two-light windows on either side of the three eastern bays of the presbytery which has on the south side a double piscina. The large east window with traces of inner lacework tracery but lacking its head is a 15th century insertion replacing three original lancets.

The interior of the priory church at Beauly. Note the piscina for a nave altar on the right.

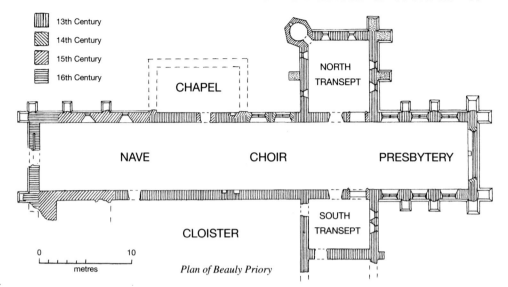

13th Century
14th Century
15th Century
16th Century

CHAPEL

NORTH
TRANSEPT

NAVE   CHOIR   PRESBYTERY

SOUTH
TRANSEPT

CLOISTER

0   10
metres   *Plan of Beauly Priory*

Transepts on either side of the choir are reached only by doorways, although on the south side there is an arch above the screen wall. This transept was called St Katherine's Aisle and has original lancets facing east and west. The dormitory extended south from here, with a sacristy below next to the transept and then presumably the chapter house. The north transept, re-roofed as the Kintail burial aisle in 1901, is longer and has two lancets on each side. In the 15th century it was vaulted in two bays, above which was a loft reached by the spiral staircase in the polygonal NW turret then added. On the floor is an incised slab depicting one of the Fraser chiefs slain in battle in 1544. East of the transept doorways on either side of the choir are a monument to Prior Mackenzie on the south side and an effigy of Sir Kenneth Mackenzie, d1441. See also page 15.

BERWICK-UPON-TWEED FRIARY *Augustinian*   Location Unknown

Berwick now lies in Northumberland but until officially annexed by the English Crown in 1333 was the county town of the Scottish county of Berwick as well as being a major port. The town's importance under Scottish rule in the 13th century is attested by the foundation of no less than six friaries. Berwick suffered much during the Anglo-Scottish wars of the 14th and 15th centuries and records of its friars and their houses are scarce. Nothing is known about the Augustinian friary except that it existed by 1296.

BERWICK-UPON-TWEED FRIARY *Carmelite*   NT 999526 At south end of town

In 2001 slight possible traces were found at Palace Green of a Carmelite house founded in 1270 by John de Grey.

BERWICK-UPON-TWEED FRIARY *Dominican*   NT 999526 North end of town

The Dominican house founded in 1260 and last mentioned in 1343 lay near Northumberland Avenue, its location outside the northern medieval town walls making it very vulnerable every time the Scots or English besieged Berwick. Here in November 1292 John Balliol was proclaimed as Edward I of England's puppet King of Scotland.

BERWICK-UPON-TWEED FRIARY *Franciscan*   NT 998535   North end of town

Alexander II is said to have founded the Franciscan friary in the early 1230s, It lay in the Low Greens area, just inside the northern walls of the medieval town.

BERWICK-UPON-TWEED FRIARY *Friars of the Sack*   NT 997529   See below

The Friars of the Sack are thought to have occupied a plot in Love Lane on the SW side of the town near the medieval bridge over the Tweed. In 1274 the Council of Lyons forbade this order to take on any recruits so that their communities died out by the early 14th century. In Berwick they were authorised in 1284 to sell their plot to the Dominicans, but it appears that the transfer may never have taken place, perhaps because the more numerous Dominicans thought that they needed a much larger precinct.

BERWICK-UPON-TWEED FRIARY *Trinitarian*   Location Unknown

The Trinitarians were the first friars to arrive in Berwick, their friary or hospital here being founded in 1214 by King William the Lion. By 1488 the Berwick Trinitarians were subject to control by the friary at Peebles. Their property here only seems to have fallen into secular hands at the Scottish Reformation of 1559-60, surviving the closure of English friaries in 1538 since although Berwick was then held by England it was treated as an anomaly, and the laws of England did not automatically apply to it.

BERWICK-UPON-TWEED PRIORY *Cistercian Nuns*   Out to the west of the town

During the course of Edward III's victory over the Scots on Hallidon Hill in 1335 a nearby nunnery was badly damaged. The king made a grant to it as a thanksgiving. The nuns were accused of dissolute living in the reign of Robert III and the house dissolved, its possessions worth £20 per annum being donated by the king to help the canons at Dryburgh recover from the burning of their abbey by Richard II of England in 1385.

The west doorway of Brechin Cathedral

BLANTYRE PRIORY
Lanarkshire   *Augustinians*
NS 686594   12km SE of Glasgow

In woodland above the west side of the River Clyde opposite the ruins of Bothwell Castle are slight traces of a priory of the Holy Rood for Augustinian canons founded in the 1240s by Patrick, Earl of Dunbar. Part of a retaining north-facing wall survives, above which seems to have stood the rectangular building shown on McGibbon & Ross's plan as the Prior's House. Traces can also be made out of the thick walled tower which stood by the cliff edge further south. They suggest that the priory church lay to the west of it and that there was a cloister to the north of that.

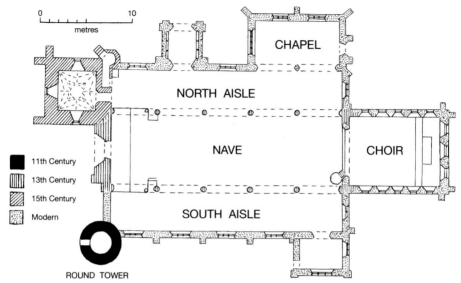

Plan of Brechin Cathedral

BRECHIN CATHEDRAL Angus *Secular Canons* NO 396601 SW side of town

There are no remains of a church built here in the mid 12th century, when David established the episcopal see, which in ground area was the smallest in Scotland, hence the comparatively modest size of the cathedral, which is about 47m long and dedicated to the Holy Trinity. An earlier relic, however, left over from a Culdee monastic settlement here, is the fine 11th century round tower at the SW corner. Rising 26m high, not including the later spire, and 4.5m in diameter at the base, it has a doorway on the west side set 2m off the ground for security and with a Crucifixion scene on the lintel.

Of the 13th century are the multi-shafted west doorway and the five bay arcades with clerestory windows set over the circular piers. The choir is also of that period but was abandoned after the Reformation and the eastern half of it has been rebuilt above the level of the sills of the lancet windows with internal shafting. The outer walls of the aisles date from a restoration of 1806, when the remains of north and south transepts were removed. On the north side a 20th century chapel of two bays now stands on the site of the transept, and a porch has been added further west, whilst a vestry has been added on the south side. At the NW corner is a fine 15th century tower of four stages with the lowest vaulted. It has a spire within a crenellated parapet and there is a smaller spire over the staircase turret on the NE corner. The nave contains an 8th century Pictish cross-slab from Aldbar and other old stones, plus a 9th or 10th century Northumbrian cross-slab and a heraldic slab of Bishop George Shoreswood, d1463. See also page 19.

Brechin: round tower doorway

The west doorway at Cambuskenneth

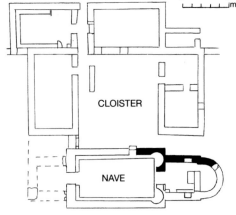

Plan of the priory at Brough of Birsay

BROUGH OF BIRSAY Orkney HY 242284 Island off NW end of mainland

Within a walled enclosure, the southern part of which formed a graveyard, on an island linked by a causeway to the mainland at low tide, are the lower parts of an early 12th century church consisting of a nave with an apsed chancel and slight traces of an intended west tower. There are circular altar recesses in the eastern corners of the nave and windows remain in the chancel and apse. The apse was later divided off from the rest of the chancel to make a tiny sacristy. No historical records of a monastery here have survived, but dating also probably from the 12th century are three small ranges set around a court or cloister about 8m by 10m on the north side of the nave. Crosswalls define a passage leading from the court NW corner between what are assumed to have been a kitchen and refectory, whilst the NE corner has a reredorter serving a dormitory over a chapter house in the east range. This was probably a small Benedictine priory.

CAMBUSKENNETH ABBEY Stirlingshire *Augustinian* NS 809939 E of Stirling

David I founded this abbey dedicated to St Mary in 1147 for Augustinian canons from Arras in France. It was alternatively known as the abbey of Stirling, and the royal castle lay barely 2km to the west. Robert Bruce's great victory of 1314 over the English was fought just 2km to the south. Representatives of the burghs are first recorded as participating in a Scottish parliament in the one that King Robert held within the abbey in 1326. About that time the king's sister Christina was married to Andrew Moray in the abbey church. Later parliaments also met here and during one of them the earls, barons, burgesses and free tenants famously granted a "tenth penny" to the king.

The English pillaged the abbey during David II's reign and in 1378 the abbey was said to be in a poor condition with its "choir greatly ruined". The abbey was favoured by the Stewart kings and in 1408 the abbot was mitred. Moved into the tower are fragments of Tournai marble from a tomb of James III, (murdered after his defeat nearby in 1488) and his consort Margaret of Denmark. Notable 16th century abbots were Patrick Pantar, secretary to James V, and Alexander Mylne, first President of the College of Justice. The buildings were sacked by Protestant reformers in 1559. The Erskine family then took control of the lands. Together with those of Dryburgh Abbey and Inchmahome Priory they were made into a temporal lordship for John, 2nd Earl of Mar in 1604-6.

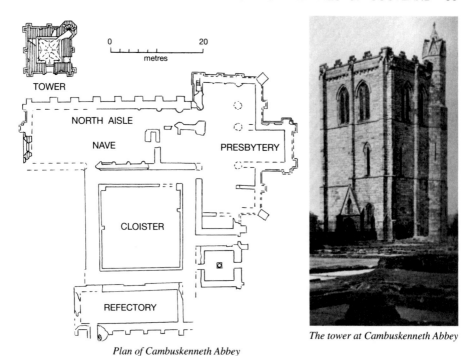

TOWER

NORTH AISLE

NAVE

PRESBYTERY

CLOISTER

REFECTORY

0   20
metres

Plan of Cambuskenneth Abbey

The tower at Cambuskenneth Abbey

The only standing parts of the church are the west doorway and the detached tower of c1300 to the north. The tower is 20m high and has a polygonal turret at the NE corner and buttresses at the other corners and in the middle of each side, the southern one rising over the apex of a centrally placed doorway. The single and paired lancet windows are all restored and there is a flat roof in place of the original saddleback-roofed caphouse. Footings, some of them reconstruction work of the 1860s, mark out an eight bay long nave with a heavily buttressed north aisle and a short presbytery extending two narrow bays beyond the pairs of chapels east of each transept. Three bays of 13th century blind arcading remaining on the south side of the nave do not correspond with the likely positions of the vanished piers of the aisle arcade. A refectory lay on the south side of a cloister about 24m square and the east range had a sacristy next to the transept, then a slype or passage, and then a square chapter house with a rib-vault supported by a central column. About 50m further east are footings of the vaulted basement of what is assumed to have been the infirmary. Another building has been traced 30m to the south. See photo on page 22.

CANONBIE PRIORY   Dumfries   *Augustinian*   NY 395764   12km NE of Gretna

A monument to the Reverend James Donaldson, d1854, lies in a 13th century round-arched tomb recess adorned with dogtooth which is the only remaining relic of an Augustinian priory founded in the 12th century by Turgis de Rosdale with canons froim Jedburgh. It lies east of a mausoleum in the graveyard of the church of 1821 by the east bank of the River Esk. Set at the bottom of the Debateable Land occupied by the Armstrongs, the priory was vulnerable to English raiding parties and was abandoned in the early 16th century.

COLDINGHAM PRIORY   Borders   *Benedictine*   NT 904659   East side of village

Around the year 1100 King Edgar attended the dedication of a new church built by the Benedictine monks of Durham on lands recently donated by the king upon or near which which had formerly stood a double monastery for both monks and nuns founded by St Aebbe c660. It may not have been until the 1130s that Durham sent up enough monks for form an independent priory. During the period 1189-1212 Bertram, prior of Durham was encouraging donations towards building a larger new church at Coldingham, the east end of which still remains. Work upon it seems to have been delayed by an attack by King John in 1216. Communications between the Coldingham community and the mother house at Durham became difficult during the Wars of Independence although it was not until 1478 that Durham abandoned all attempts to control what went on at Coldingham. An attempt by James III to refound the priory as a Chapel Royal foundered with the king's defeat and death in 1488. The priory was burnt by the Earl of Hertford in 1542 and again during his further campaigns of 1544 and 1545. In the 1570s Alexander Home, later Earl of Home, got himself appointed as commendator, and the lands of the priory, together with those of Jedburgh Abbey were made into a lordship for him in 1606. Cromwell's troops wrecked the church in 1648 but the east end was patched up for parish worship in 1661 and still serves for that purpose.

The present church is eight bays long and aisleless. Original are the east and north walls with lancets set high up which internally form part of an upper arcade with a continuous gallery, and the boldly projecting east corner buttresses with angle-rolls. Externally the lancets have keeled rolls, shaft-rings halfway up and capitals with crockets and stiff-leaf. The external blind arcading set over a string course above a chamfered plinth has round arches with chevrons and shafts with waterleaf capitals, probably of the 1190s. Excavations during the 1850s, when the west and south walls of 1661 were rebuilt and the porch added, revealed footings of the church of 1100, which had an east apse and a west tower. The lower parts remain of a 13th century south transept with three east chapels and a huge SE corner staircase turret, but nothing remains of the north transept or the aisled nave six bays long which would have produced a building about 65m long.

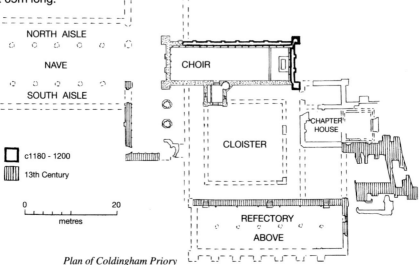

NORTH AISLE

NAVE

SOUTH AISLE

CHOIR

CHAPTER HOUSE

CLOISTER

☐ c1180 - 1200

▦ 13th Century

0   20
metres

REFECTORY
ABOVE

Plan of Coldingham Priory

The east end of the church at Coldingham Priory

Arcading inside the choir at Coldingham

Very unusually, the cloister at Coldingham lay to the south of the east end rather than beside the nave. This arose because the existing east end (or choir and presbytery) replaced the whole of the much smaller early 12th century church. Enough remains of the early 13th century refectory north wall to show that its undercroft had central piers carrying vaulting two bays wide and seven bays long. It had two doorways facing the cloister. To the south of the meagre remains of the chapter house, which seems to have had a western vestibule, are more massive walls which supported the reredorter projecting east from the dormitory on the upper level of the east range.

COLDSTREAM PRIORY   Borders *Cistercian Nuns*   NT 844397   SE end of town

The town was created by Sir John Hamilton, former commendator of the vanished Cistercian nunnery founded in the mid 12th century by Gospatrick, Earl of Dunbar. In 1296 the nuns were given 700 sheep after the English army camped on its lands.

COUPAR ANGUS ABBEY   Perthshire *Cistercian*   NO 223398   South side of town

The only standing building of the Cistercian abbey founded by Malcolm IV in the 1160s is a 15th century gateway of two upper storeys over a vaulted pend and with a stepped diagonal SE corner buttress. It lies at the SW corner of the graveyard in Queen Street which accompanies the Abbey Church of 1859-60. Amongst later monuments in the church are a worn effigy of a 15th century knight, a head of a man, and a grave slab with a relief of Abbot John Schanwel, d1506. Another small effigy and various architectural fragments are scattered around outside and two old stone coffins lie beside the gatehouse. The abbey church was dedicated in 1233. The abbey was suppressed in 1560. The lands then producing an income of £5,590 Scots per annum (the largest income of any Cistercian abbey in Scotland) were made into a temporal barony for James Elphinstone, who thus became Lord Coupar, the town then made a burgh of barony.

CROSSRAGUEL ABBEY Ayrshire *Cluniac* NS 275083 3km SW of Maybole

In the early 13th century Duncan, Earl of Carrick handed over lands and custody of four parish churches to the Cluniac monks of Paisley, intending that they would colonise a daughter house at Crossraguel. Initially only a small chapel was established here but this was upgraded to an abbey on the order of William de Bondington, Bishop of Glasgow in 1244. The community could elect its own abbots but was subject to visitations by the mother house. Still surviving are details of a visitation in 1370 by John, Abbot of Paisley which resulted in the elderly Abbot Roger of Crossraguel resigning and retiring to the abbey of Dunfermline and Abbot Nicholas being elected in his place. In 1404 Robert III issued a charter confirming the abbey in all its possessions, which were made into a regality making the abbot all-powerful in Carrick and the greatest lord in Ayrshire. About that time the community had ten monks.

A 16th century screen wall surmounted by a double bellcote divides almost equally in two an aisleless church 50m long. The nave was once used by lay parishioners but latterly used as a Lady Chapel with two altars against the screen wall. The south wall and west corners, plus footings of a former north transept are all that remain of the mid 13th century church wrecked during the wars of the 1290s. The west doorway and north wall with several two-light windows and buttresses are 14th century, although the last but one window is 15th century. In the NE corner is the tomb-slab of Egilia Blair, Lady Row, d1530. The choir to the east of the screen was rebuilt in the late 15th century as a structure of five bays with a polygonal east apse with four-light windows, although the western part of the south wall is 14th century work. There are remains of sedilia and a piscina in a position which indicates that the altar was once further east instead of set back as now to allow a tiny sacristy behind it.

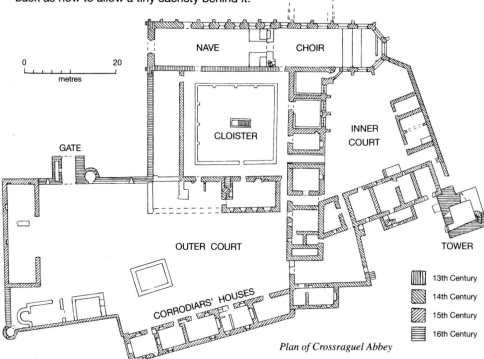

Plan of Crossraguel Abbey

View of Crossraguel Abbey from the gatehouse

The cloister and the buildings around it are also 14th century but were mostly re-modelled in the 15th century, and the sacristy south of the choir and the chapter house beyond it are entirely of that later period. Both these rooms have three-light eastern windows and the chapter house is vaulted in two bays by two with a clustered central pier. The sacristy is also vaulted and has on the north wall traces of a 13th century arch from the original crossing to a lost south transept. Above a window with a mullion and transom lighted a room divided off from the original dormitory. In the 15th century a new staircase was built to the dormitory on the site of the treasury south of the chapter house. There is a latrine drain at the south end of the east range. The south range con-tained the refectory, west of which was the kitchen, of which little survives. There was no proper west range, just a parlour beside the nave. To the east of the east range lay an almost triangular court with the abbot's house on the SE side. The square four storey tower house adjoining the east corner was added in the 1530s to serve either as a resi-dence for the last abbot, William Kennedy, a younger brother of the 2nd Earl of Cassilis, or to provide rooms for the 3rd Earl, a minor then in the custody of Abbot William.

It was probably William's nephew and successor Quintin Kennedy, titled commenda-tor from 1560, who closed off the north side of the outer court to the south and south-west of the cloister with a new wall with a gatehouse with a staircase in a circular turret on the east side leading to two upper rooms suitable for accommodation for adminis-trative officials. The turret has a square caphouse with chequered corbelling below the eaves of its roof, and the gate-tower itself had a corbelled parapet. Of the same period is the circular turret at the court SW corner with a corbelled out upper storey forming a dovecot. North of it is 15th century barn, and east of it are footings of bakehouses. On the south side of the outer court are footings of a row of 15th century houses for corrodiars, who were people living in retirement in the abbey in return usually for hav-ing earlier provided funds or important services in an hour of need. Each one has a fireplace, latrine and a pair of windows with seats in the embrasures. There were still corrodiars living here in 1589, when they agreed to take out new leases from the then commendator, John Vaux. Payments made in 1592 suggest that two or three monks were also still then in residence at the abbey. Twenty five years later the abbey lands were handed over to the bishops of Dunblane.

CULROSS ABBEY   Fife   *Cistercian*   NS 989863   Above north side of village

This abbey was founded c1215 by Malcolm, Earl of Fife for Cistercian monks from Kinloss. The aisleless nave was originally intended as a choir for lay brothers as was usual in Cistercian houses. The 13th century south wall still remains but the rest of the nave was demolished c1500 under Abbot Andrew Masoun since there were by then no lay brothers left. A tower was then raised above a vestibule enclosed by a former rood screen on the west and a pulpitum on the east. The tower doorway has probably been reset from the nave west wall. At the tower top original corbelling supports a parapet of 1823. Adjoining the tower NW corner is a circular stair turret and the stub of the west wall of an intended short north aisle or chapel of c1500 probably never completed.

The monastic choir east of the tower dates from the late 13th to early 14th century. It has transepts with pairs of eastern chapels, although the northern one was entirely rebuilt in the 17th century when the Bruce family vault of 1642 was added beyond its northern chapel. Most of the south transept was refaced in the restoration of 1905, when the 15th century windows of the main body were re-opened and renewed. The south transept has an original 13th century arch with keeled shafts between it and the crossing. East of this transept is a low 15th century arch with the de Quincy arms on the hoodmould facing the northern chapel. Originally there was an effigy under the arch. The north transept arch is at least partly 14th century and east of it is an arch over fragmentary effigies of John Stewart, Lord of Lorn, d1445 and his wife. In the Bruce vault are effigies of Sir George Bruce of Carnock, d1625 and his wife with kneeling figures of their children and other Bruce memorials, including a gravestone of Edward, d1565.

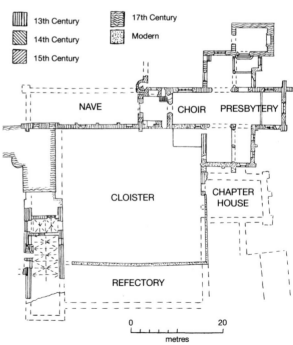

The west range at Culross Abbey   *Plan of Culross Abbey*

Culross Abbey from the SE

The placing of the cloister on steeply sloping ground to the south necessitated lofty and massively constructed vaulted undercrofts to enable the main rooms such as the chapter house in the east range and the refectory in the south range to be located at cloister level. The manse of 1637 with an additional third storey of 1752 has replaced the northern part of the west range. The part of the range still surviving has a rib-vaulted entrance passage and the north end of a vaulted refectory for the lay-brothers, their dormitory being above and barrel-vaulted rooms below. The kitchen was perhaps below the monks' refectory. Of the walls at cloister level of the south and east ranges just a tantalising fragment remains of the west facade of the chapter house with a central doorway flanked by windows. The undercroft below has a row of piers down the middle but only one vaulting cell now remains. A projection two bays wide extending one bay and having big corner buttresses supported the chapter house east wall. Another projection further east formed part of the rere-dorter.

CUPAR FRIARY   Fife   *Dominican*   NO 377146   East side of town centre

In 1519 the expanding Dominican friary in St Andrews forming part of the university there was allowed to take over the possessions of a much older sister house in Cupar, probably founded in the 13th century by one of the earls of Fife. The last remaining part of the church at Cupar was removed for the creation of St Catherine Street in the 19th century. The Episcopal church of St James stands close to the site of the friary.

DALMULLIN PRIORY   Ayrshire   Gilbertine   Uncertain location 2km E of Ayr

Walter Fitzalan invited a part of Gilbertines up from Lincolnshire to establish a priory of St Mary beside the north bank of the River Ayr. The Gilbertines returned to England in 1238 and the priory's lands were then transferred to the abbey of Paisley.

DEER ABBEY   Aberdeenshire   *Cistercian*   NJ 968481   3km west of Mintlaw

In 1219 Cistercian monks from Kinloss were established here by William Comyn, Earl of Buchan. It superseded a Celtic monastery probably located where now lies the parish church of Old Deer 1km to the east, from which there survives the Book of Deer now at Cambridge University Library. William had married Marjorie, heiress of the Celtic chiefs of Buchan, who were the main patrons of the older monastery, some of their gifts during the 11th and 12th centuries being recorded on the margins of the Gospels in the Book of Deer. It is likely that the last few Celtic monks joined the new abbey, since only three monks are recorded as being sent over from Kinloss. In the 13th century two of the abbots (who eventually became mitred) were men sent up from Melrose, but both retired down south again, one finding the Buchan climate not to his taste, and the other finding that the monks at Deer lacked the courteous charm of the brethren at Melrose.

The abbey lands were amongst those in Buchan devastated by King Robert in 1308 but he eventually made up for this by adding to them. In 1537 the abbots of Kinloss and Glenluce paid a visitation and issued a charter of mitigation, allowing the Cistercian rules to be interpreted less strictly at Deer. The abbot was ordered to repair the buildings, particularly the choir of the church. In 1543 , when there were still fourteen monks at Deer, Robert Keith, a younger brother of the 4th Earl Marischal was appointed abbot. He remained a layman, administering the lands and revenues and left the internal management of the house to Prior Robert Stevenson. In 1551 another Robert Keith became commendator or lay abbot, despite being just a boy of fifteen and in 1587 the abbey lands were erected into a barony of Altrie for this Robert. His nephew, another Robert Keith (or Benholm) seized the abbey in 1590 and was only dislodged when his kinsman the Earl Marishal arrived with forty musketeers borrowed from the city of Aberdeen. The buildings were dismantled about that time. The ruins were cleared up in 1809 but much of the church was destroyed in 1854 for the construction of the Ferguson Mausoleum which was removed in the 1930s after the abbey site was acquired by the Roman Catholic church and placed in State care.

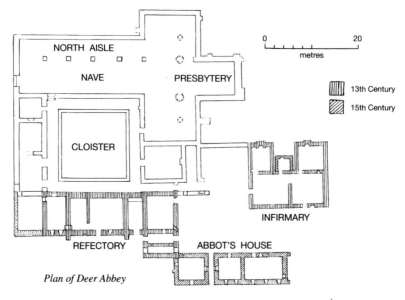

Plan of Deer Abbey

Deer Abbey from the SE

Only foundations remain of the church, which had transepts each with two east chapels, a presbytery extending another two bays further east, and a nave with a five bay arcade opening into a north aisle. A single aisled nave is uncommon in a Cistercian church and all the buildings here were modest in scale. To the south was a cloister about 20m square, still with footings of the arcading dividing the four lean-to roofed alleys from the inner garth. The west range shows no obvious signs of being designed to accommodate lay brothers and may be of later date. The chapter house lay beside the south transept without the usual sacristy between them. South of it lay a passage and then the parlour, beyond which are the latrine pits of the reredorter serving the dormitory above. Slightly more remains of the south range, where there was a kitchen and the refectory lay on an upper floor, and of the abbot's house extending east from the reredorter SE corner. This building is later medieval and contained several rooms over three vaulted storage or service rooms. East of the chapter house lies the infirmary with rooms with fireplaces extending north from a two main chambers on the south side.

DIRLETON FRIARY   Lothian   *Trinitarian*   Location Unknown

The Trinitarians held a chapel of St Andrew here from the 15th century until at least 1567. Its lands had been annexed to the Crown by 1588 and its location is unknown.

Deer Abbey from the east

DORNOCH CATHEDRAL   Highland   *Secular Canons*   NH 798898   In town centre

In the 1150s David I established a bishopric of Caithness based at Halkirk in attempt to bring the Norse-controlled northern part of Scotland more under his influence. A new cathedral at Dornoch, rather more easily accessible from the south by virtue of its coastal location, was begun immediately after Gilbert de Moravia was appointed bishop c1223. The choir must have been complete by 1239, when the bones of Bishop Adam were brought over from Halkirk for burial here, and Bishop Gilbert was himself buried within it in 1245. William, Earl of Sutherland is said to have been buried in the south transept in 1248. The forty seasoned oaks from Darnaway Forest granted by Edward I of England in 1291 probably indicate when the nave was ready to be roofed. It was probably this part of the building that in 1428 was said to be "collapsed in its fabric, desolate and destitute and in need of costly repairs", resulting in a papal indulgence being granted to those contributing to the costs. In 1570 the cathedral was burned by the Master of Caithness and Mackay of Strathnaver. The nave was still roofless in 1605, when the arcade on the north side of the nave collapsed in a gale. The Earl of Sutherland and his brother Robert had the choir and transepts repaired for parochial worship in 1614-22, and other repairs are recorded in 1714, 1728, 1772-5 and 1816.

The existing church has an external length of about 40m. It has a central tower and a slated broach-spire within a parapet above remarkably wide crossing arches. The transepts and chancel are of similar length, but the transepts have two bays, whilst the chancel has three bays and three east lancets. These parts have mid 13th century walling. The clustered crossing piers and arches are original and a piscina survives in the chancel. The lancets, doorways, corner buttresses, plaster vaults, the porches beyond each transept and the modest vestries in the angles between the chancel and transepts are all of the restoration of 1835-7. Internally the lancets are set in blind arcading.

Old postcard showing the south side of Dornoch Cathedral unobstructed by trees

13th century effigy of a knight in Dornoch Cathedral

The four bay nave is entirely of 1835-7, although the five-light west window with Y-tracery probably reproduces a 15th century one and it contains an effigy of a knight in chain mail said to be of Richard de Moravia, c1245. No other medieval monuments or furnishings have survived, although there are several 18th to 20th century monuments in the chancel and in the south transept, where the Earls of Sutherland were buried. Neither of the medieval aisles were re-instated in the 1835-7 restoration but the east responds of the arcades remain. The south arcade survived to the late 18th century. On the east side of the north transept there survives the roof raggle of a sacristy removed in 1813. It appears that the tower may have been taller until remodelled in 1714.

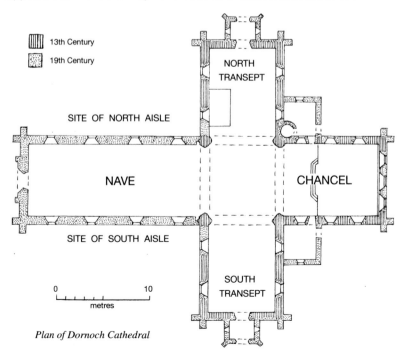

Plan of Dornoch Cathedral

DRYBURGH ABBEY   Borders   *Premonstratensian*   NT 591307   5km SE of Melrose

According to the Chronicle of Melrose Abbey a group of Premonstratensian canons arrived here in 1152 from Alnwick to establish a community with Hugh de Morville, Constable of Scotland, who had donated suitable lands in 1150, as founder. King David I has also been claimed as founder because of his endowments to it. Adam, the third abbot was a noted preacher but transferred to the Carthusians in 1190. The names of many of the other abbots are known. In the 1260s, during the time of Abbot Oliver, Dryburgh sent out canons to Ireland to found daughter houses at Drumcross and Woodburn, and in the 1290s the prior was one of the hundred commissioners appointed to assist Edward I of England in chosing who should be king of Scotland.

In 1322 the abbey was burned by the retreating forces of Edward II of England. King Robert aided the repairs and the Bishop of Glasgow handed over the church at Maxton but the canons were still appealing for money for repairs in the 1330s. In 1355 Abbot Andrew saved the abbey from another burning by English forces, when he, along with other local abbots submitted to Edward III at Roxburgh and Edward Balliol resigned his claim to the Scottish Crown. It was about this time that the noted scholar Ralph Strode lived in the abbey before being send by David II to study at Oxford. Strode travelled widely in Europe, befriended Chaucer and opposed the heretical views of John Wycliffe.

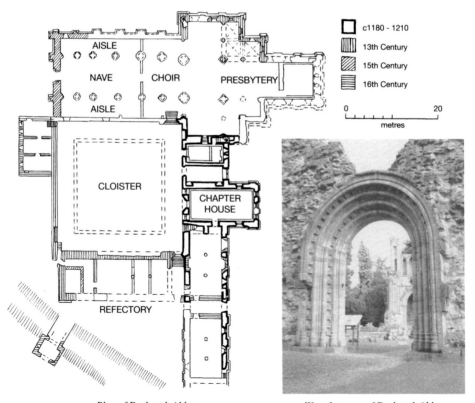

Plan of Dryburgh Abbey   *West doorway of Dryburgh Abbey*

The chapter house entrance facade at Dryburgh Abbey

The abbey was burned again in 1385, this time by Richard II of England. In the early 15th century the revenues of a small convent of Cistercian nuns near Berwick which was then suppressed were handed over to Dryburgh to help rebuild the ruined abbey. No abbots were appointed after the dawn of the 16th century. A series of commendators held the lands, the first of whom, Andrew Forman, became Archbishop of St Andrews in 1514, and the third was David Hamilton who held the revenues of Dryburgh, along with the impoverished bishopric of Argyll. The abbey seems to have suffered in the Earl of Surrey's raids of 1523, and it was again burned (except the church) by English forces in 1544, who also took away all the abbey's animals and supplies of corn. By this time the Erskine family were hereditary commendators, administering an estate said to be worth £912 a year. In 1561 one of them signed a document along with the sub-prior and eight other canons. By 1584 there were just four canons left and a document of 1600 refers to "all the convent theirof being now deceisset".

The church, dedicated to St Mary, had an aisled six bay nave and transepts with pairs of eastern chapels, the inner of which extended for a second bay beside the presbytery. The canons' choir stalls lay in the eastern two bays of the nave with a screen to the west of them. All the arcades are reduced to pier bases except for a fairly complete section of good 13th century work around the rib-vaulted northern chapels, where the novelist Sir Walter Scott lies buried. Enough remains here to show that the north transept had two levels of triplets of lancets and bullet marks remain from the English attack of 1544. One of the vault bosses depicts Christ in Majesty with the right hand raised in blessing and a book in the left hand. Little remains of the 13th century east end of the presbytery, the two eastern bays of which were later divided off to create a chapel or large vestry. Not much remains of the aisle walls but there is a fine round-arched doorway of c1200 adorned with dogtooth towards the NE corner of cloister (see page 7). There are traces of the night stair in the better preserved south transept, where some of the lower walling is 12th century and each eastern chapel retains a piscina. What remains of the west front is all 15th century work, with a good round-arched central doorway with fleurons on the second and fourth of four moulded orders.

Eastern chapels of the north transept at Dryburgh Abbey   *Dunbar: friary tower converted to dovecot*

The cloister at Dryburgh is 27m square. There are no signs of a medieval western range, although a 16th century building now lies on the northern half of where it would have been. In the SW corner is a lavatorium for the monks to use before ascending to the upper floor refectory in the south range, now very fragmentary. The east range, on the other hand, is amongst the most complete of any abbey in Scotland as a result on continued domestic occupation during the 17th century. The lower storey is mostly late 12th century work in the round-arched Late-Norman style with broad pilaster buttresses on the east side. A library and vestry and a parlour form two narrow chambers between the transept and the chapter house. This room projects further east and has triple east lancets, an arcade of seats, a barrel-vault, and a fine entrance facade with two-light windows on each side of a splendid central doorway. There are traces of late 12th century mural painting. South of here are the warming house with an inserted 14th century fireplace, and the novices day room with an original 13th century fireplace. A passage leads out eastwards between these rooms and above was the canons' dormitory. The internal dividing walls here are 16th century. An extra third storey upper room was added against the transept after the destruction of the original roof in the attack of 1322. Just to the SW of the cloister buildings is a small 16th century gatehouse straddling a water course.

DUMFRIES FRIARY   Dumfries   *Franciscan*   NX 970761   West side of the town

The church of the Franciscan friary founded in 1265 by Devorguilla, Lady of Galloway was in 1306 the scene of the fatal stabbing of John Comyn of Dalswinton by Robert Bruce after the two met there for a conference. The name Friars Vennel commemorates the site.

DUNBAR FRIARY   Lothian   *Carmelite*   NT 680787   SW side of the town

According to Spottiswode this friary was founded in 1263 by Patrick, 7th Earl of Dunbar. A freemasons' lodge is said to lie on the site.

DUNBAR FRIARY   Lothian   *Trinitarians*   NT 679788   On west side of the town

The last remaining part of the friary founded in the 1240s by Christiana Bruce, Countess of Dunbar on the pilgrims' coastal route to St Andrews is the lower part of a later medieval tower placed on crosswalls defining a passage between the nave and choir of the church. Excavations showed that the church had a total length of 39m and found in the choir some remains of a new floor of c1500 using yellow and green tiles from the Netherlands. Yet within less than thirty years the community had died out. The tower north and south walls are carried on plain round arches on moulded imposts but the east and west walls have been rebuilt to provide nesting boxes for pigeons and have lost their former arches. Before conversion into a dovecot the tower must have been considerably higher. The friars also looked after the Maison Dieu Hospital in Dunbar.

Dunblane Cathedral from the SE

DUNBLANE CATHEDRAL   Stirlingshire   *Secular Canons*   NN 781013   W of town

Legend has it that St Blane built a church here c600 within a Pictish fort beside the river. Certainly Dunblane was a monastic centre by the 9th century. The first certain mention of a bishop here is in 1155. Only the tower remains of a new church begun about that time. When the Dominican friar Clement was elected bishop in 1233 the church at Dunblane was said to be roofless and the diocesan finances in disarray. Moving the cathedral to Inchaffray was considered but after a papal mandate was issued in 1237 a new cathedral was begun at Dunblane. It appears that the whole of the existing building was laid out in one operation after which the five bay range on north side of the choir was completed first to provide a treasury and chapel over a chapter house and sacristy, then the nave was completed, and finally the choir, although it is possible that the choir was completed first and then drastically remodelled two generations later.

The cathedral is dedicated to St Blane and St Laurence. By the 1550s it was served by a dean, precentor, chancellor, treasurer, archdeacon, nine prebendaries and twelve choral chaplains. In June 1559 the Earl of Argyll ordered the cathedral to be purged of all "monuments of idolatrye" and by 1562 it was served by a reformed minister. In the 1570s only the choir remained in use as a parish church, being eventually filled with galleries to take all of the townsfolk. Not much of the nave roof remained by 1622. Only the tower and the bays of the south aisle east of it in use for burials are shown roofed in Slezer's view of 1693. The choir was re-roofed in 1860-2 and restored in the 1870s, and then from 1886 onwards the nave was restored and eventually brought back into use.

The tower has a short spire surrounded by a parapet of c1500 bearing the arms of Bishop James Chisholm but the lower parts are 12th century work. It may have sat in a south transeptal position in relation to the church of that period although there is certain evidence it was then attached to anything. It now stands nearly halfway along the south aisle, projecting both inside and outside it at an awkward angle, having a north doorway at a higher level, a spiral staircase, and windows on all four sides at fourth storey level.

Old picture of the west front of Dunblane Cathedral

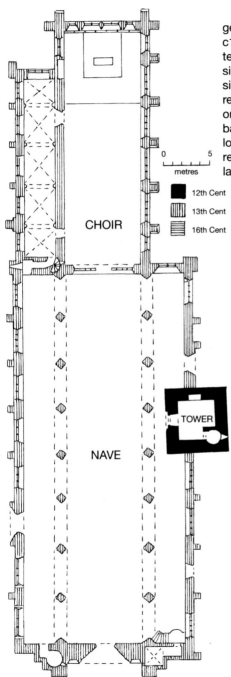

CHOIR

■ 12th Cent

▥ 13th Cent

▤ 16th Cent

0   5

metres

TOWER

NAVE

Plan of Dunblane Cathedral

East windows over the chancel arch suggest that the aisleless choir was completed c1300 to a greater height than originally intended. It has a four-light east window and six bays of three-light windows on the south side. The tracery is of 1889-93 and may not reproduce the original design. There is only one north window because the other five bays are flanked by the sacristy range, the lower level of which is vaulted and also has restored windows composed of triplets of lancets under an outer arch.

The aisled nave has eight bay arcades and the aisles have windows in the form of four grouped lancets. There is a good doorway on the north side but only a modest one on the south side. The piers have four major and four minor shafts and the arches are of a complex moulded section. It appears that lower arcades were originally intended, along with vaults over the aisles. Some of the clerestory windows have plate tracery and bar tracery, and the latter can hardly be earlier than c1280. The west front has a single blind arch on either side of a deeply recessed central doorway surmounted by three tall two-light windows and huge buttresses in line with the arcades. One buttress has a spiral staircase within it and the other the tiny vaulted chapel of St Clement.

In addition to adding the tower top Bishop Chisholm enlarged two windows of the north aisle west end to accommodate a chapel of St Blaise and the Holy Blood, added a parapet to the choir, and provided the fine set of choir stalls with canopies and misericords that now lie against the nave west wall. The cathedral has many fine 19th and 20th century furnishings and much stained glass which cannot be described here. The oldest monuments include effigies of two 13th century bishops, one thought to be Clement, d1258, and a 13th century knight, possibly an earl of Strathearn, with his wife, and a pair of elaborately decorated 8th or 9th century cross-slabs.

DUNDEE FRIARY   Angus   *Franciscan*   NO 402304   In middle of city centre

A cemetery beside Barrack Street contains a very slight platform which is probably the site of the Franciscan friary where in 1309 the Scottish clergy held a meeting and declared their support for Robert Bruce as King of Scotland, having forgiven him for the sacrilege of a murder committed in the friary at Dumfries. This friary was founded c1284-9, burned by the English in 1335, sacked by reformers as early as 1543, and was in the hands of the town council by 1560, having possibly been burned in 1548.

DUNDRENNAN ABBEY   Galloway   *Cistercian*   NX 749475   7km SE Kirkcudbright

Cistercian monks from Rievaulx established this community in the 1140s. David I, d1153, Fergus, Lord of Galloway, d1161, and St Malachy, Bishop of Armagh are all claimed as founders. A plausible suggestion is that Malachy brought the Cistercians to lands made available by Fergus at Soulseat in 1148, and that Premonstratensian canons took over that site after the Cistercians moved to Dundrennan c1156. The eastern parts of the church may have been completed by the mid 1160s, when work was begun on the cloister and its buildings but medieval records of the abbey are scarce. The buildings were said to be in a poor state in 1529 as a result of both neglect and English attacks and in 1543 the west end of the nave was ruinous. The eastern parts of the church remained in use for parish worship until 1742. Repairs wee made in 1838 and shortly afterwards the ruins were taken into State care.

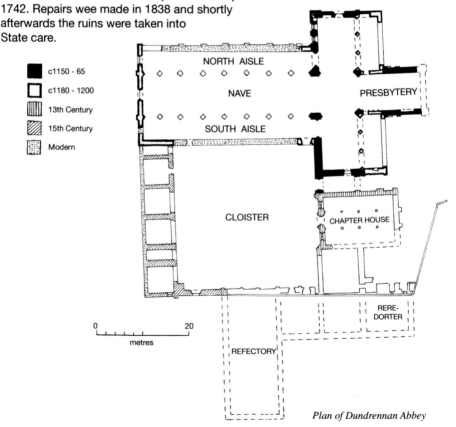

c1150 - 65
c1180 - 1200
13th Century
15th Century
Modern

NORTH AISLE
NAVE
PRESBYTERY
SOUTH AISLE
CLOISTER
CHAPTER HOUSE
RERE-DORTER
REFECTORY

0   20
metres

Plan of Dundrennan Abbey

The transepts of the church at Dundrennan Abbey

Only restored low walls remain of the fully aisled eight bay long nave apart from the pointed-arched west doorway of c1185-1200. The aisles also had west doorways but rebuilding in the 1840s has tampered with the evidence. There are substantial ruins of the transepts and presbytery although the latter has lost its east end. Here the three eastern chapels of each transept were additions of c1180-1200 rather than original features of the work of the 1160s since their roofs obscured the lower part of the west-ernmost clerestory windows of the older presbytery. Alan, Lord of Galloway is thought to have been buried in the NE chapel in 1234. All the chapels have lost their east walls and vaulting. They were originally separated from each other by wooden screens. Over the arches into the chapels from the transept is a triforium, a rare feature in a Cistercian church. The north transept retains its north doorway of two orders with foliage capitals, two tiers of west-facing round-arched windows with hoodmoulds on nook-shafts with bell-capitals and a pointed arch into the north aisle. The transept corners have clasping buttresses, the NW one having a spiral staircase. The presbytery has shafts for vaulting and remains of sedilia which mostly projected from the wall rather than recessed into it. There is also a very damaged double piscina.

The cloister to the south was about 31m square. The vaulted cellars on the west side are 15th century work (much repaired in 1840-3) replacing rooms originally for lay broth-ers. The refectory is known to have extended north-south from the middle of the south side, a common Cistercian practice. A doorway west of it probably led to the kitchen. Of the east range there remains a room next to the transept and then the mid 13th century chapter house, once divided by piers carrying rib vaults into a chamber three bays wide by four east to west. It has a fine entrance facade with two-light windows either side of a central doorway. Excavations have revealed the lower parts further south of the warming room and the heavily buttressed reredorter with a double south wall containing latrine slots. The slots were reduced in width during a 15th century rebuilding neces-sitated by subsidence of the artificial terracing here.

DUNFERMLINE ABBEY   Fife   *Benedictine*   NT 090873   On west side of town

Shortly after her marriage c1070 to Malcolm III (Canmore) the Saxon Princess Margaret, sister of Edgar Atheling and great-niece of Edward the Confessor, invited up a few Benedictine monks from Canterbury to establish a priory beside the royal palace. An apsed choir for the monks was added to the palace chapel in which Malcolm and Margaret were married. Previously it had just a small chancel east of a square nave-tower as marked out on the present floor. Their son David I confirmed the priory in its possessions in 1128 and had it ungraded to an abbey, after which a larger new church was built which was consecrated in 1150. Work on extending the east end in the early 13th century is assumed to have been mostly completed by 1250, when the bodies of Malcolm and the recently canonised Margaret were reinterred by the high altar.

The refectory was rebuilt in 1329, and probably also the guesthouse, following some damage being sustained from Edward I's troops in 1304. The nave remained in use as a parish church after the last few monks were dispersed in 1560. Much of the abandoned choir collapsed in 1672 and the central tower fell down in 1716. All these parts were cleared away for the construction in 1818-21 of a new cruciform parish church. The nave became just a vestibule and as early 1845 it was taken into state guardianship, since when other parts of the site have also become a state-run ancient monument. None of the many fine memorials and furnishings go back to the monastic period.

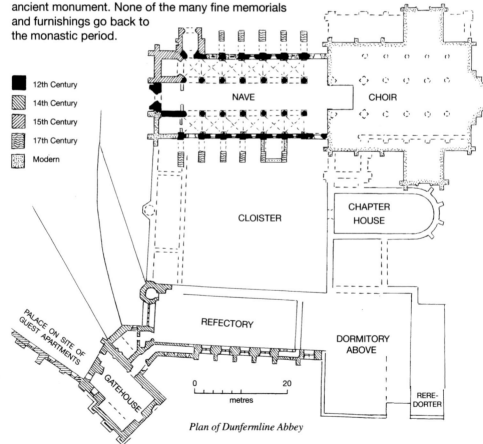

12th Century
14th Century
15th Century
17th Century
Modern

NAVE
CHOIR
CLOISTER
CHAPTER HOUSE
PALACE ON SITE OF GUEST APARTMENTS
GATEHOUSE
REFECTORY
DORMITORY ABOVE
RERE-DORTER

0   20
metres

Plan of Dunfermline Abbey

The refectory and south end of the dormitory undercroft at Dunfermline. See also pages 3, 13 & 16.

Slight traces of the eastern chapel enclosing St Margaret's shrine are all that remain of the crossing, transepts, fully aisled five bay choir, and the wide chapel added on the north side in the late 14th century. The church was once 80m long. Although fine in its details its scale was not large and the nave actually seems quite narrow. There are arcades of circular piers with spiral and chevron decoration, although there is also one compound pier. Three piers on the south side were rebuilt in the 1840s and the outer walls with their original round-arched windows between pilaster buttresses are held up on both sides by heavy flying buttresses of the 1620s. At the west end is an extra bay with a sumptuous doorway with chevrons and grotesque heads and a window of c1400 above lying between two quite different towers. The north tower of c1400, but with a machicolated parapet and spire probably of c1500, is the larger of the two. The south tower seems to have remained 12th century work until it collapsed in 1807, and everything above the lowest stage was rebuilt in 1811. The north porch was added by Abbot Richard Bothwell in the mid 15th century in front of another fine 12th century doorway of four orders with nook-shafts and chevrons. A third good doorway faces the cloister.

Little remains of the cloister about 30m square on the south side and there are only footings of the west and east ranges, the latter with a projecting and apsed chapter house and a reredorter to the east of the south end of that range. More survives of the heavily buttressed south wall of the refectory which lay over vaulted cellars. This room has a huge west window with reticulated tracery. Below its SW corner is a gateway over a steeply climbing road. This gateway links across to a long range of buildings with their lofty three storey south wall dramatically perched on the edge of a cliff. Originally the 14th century guest rooms, these apartments were frequently used as a royal palace long before the abbey was dissolved. The mullion and transom windows date from a remodelling in the 1590s for James VI's consort Anne of Denmark. The best preserved part is the kitchen at the east end. North of the church lies the much altered mid-15th century abbot's house in which one original traceried window facing the town has been discovered. An excavation at the SE corner of the precinct (which was larger than the adjacent burgh) showed that this corner was finally walled in the 14th century, having originally been defined by a widened burn and probably a bank with a fence or hedge.

DUNKELD CATHEDRAL   Perthshire   *Secular Canons*   NO 024426   West of town

Kenneth MacAlpine chose Dunkeld as the organising centre of the early Culdee monasteries and c845 made it the see of a bishop. The see then extended out to Iona, from which was brought over part of the relics of St Columba to keep them safe from Norse raids.   The bishops seem to have lapsed in favour hereditary abbots, one of them, Creathanan MacDhonochaidh, becoming an ancestor of the Scottish kings through his marriage with Malcolm II's eldest daughter Beathag. Alexander I revived the see and the first of the new bishops seems to have been Cormac, who witnessed the foundation charter of the royal abbey of Scone c1114.

A college of canons with a constitution modelled on that of Salisbury Cathedral was established in the 1230s. Bishop Geoffrey enlarged the chapter, introduced Gregorian chant and began work on a new choir in which he was buried in 1249, most of his predecessors having been buried at Inchcolm Abbey. The cathedral's position made it vulnerable to raids by unruly highland caterans. On one occasion the Donockeys invaded it during mass after Bishop Lauder imprisoned one of them. So it comes as a surprise to find that the choir contains a tomb of c1420 with a splendid effigy of the notoriously unruly Alexander Stewart, Earl of Buchan, a royal prince better known as the Wolf of Badenoch, who burned Elgin Cathedral after being defied by its bishop.

In later years a struggle between the papacy and the crown over episcopal appointments ended the practice of promoting one of the chapter. The cathedral was purged of images by reformers in 1560 and in 1571 the see was declared void, Bishop Robert Crichton having been forfeited and imprisoned. The nave has been roofless since then but a tablet on the choir records that it was re-roofed in 1600 to serve as a parish church. The choir's medieval form was reinstated in 1908 after a typical early 19th century remodelling with a lower new roof and the insertion of galleries at either end.

The roofless nave of Dunkeld Cathedral

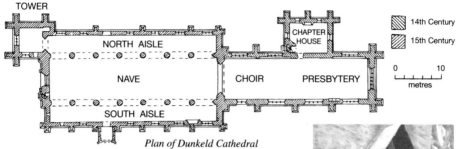

TOWER

CHAPTER HOUSE

NORTH AISLE

NAVE   CHOIR   PRESBYTERY

SOUTH AISLE

14th Century

15th Century

0   10
metres

Plan of Dunkeld Cathedral

The cathedral is over 80m long but is comparatively narrow, since it has no transepts or choir aisles and the nave aisles are of modest width. The choir has four very long bays with four-light windows with 19th century tracery. Much of the choir, including the sedilia on the south side, appears to date from a rebuilding by Bishop William Sinclair, d1337, who gained fame by defeating a force of English invaders in 1317, and whose head-less effigy lies on the north side. However, the two bays further west have 13th century blind arcading internally so the lower walls at least must be of that period. On the north side is the chapter house bearing the arms of Bish-op Lauder. The lowest level is vaulted and now serves as the Atholl mausoleum, with a pair of 17th century tombs. Alterations in 1815 resulted in the blocking of three of the upper storey windows. See photo on page 12.

Cardeny Tomb at Dunkeld

The aisled nave of seven bays has arcades of study round piers supporting moulded arches, over which is a triforium of semi-circular arches with tracery under them. The work was completed to that height by Bishop Robert de Cardeny, d1436, whose effigy lies under a fine canopy on the south side, where the eastern bays of the aisle were screened off to form the chapel of St Ninian. A chapel of St Mary lay opposite on the north side. The buttressing is more regular and complete on the south side than the north. Above the outer corners of the south aisle are octagonal turrets, and another flanks the south side of the nave west window, over which is a roundel with tracery of three cusped daggers. The main window here had flamboyant tracery and is larger than the one originally planned, resulting in various irregularities. Work on completing these parts, the clerestory and roof, and also the chapter house, must have been completed by 1464, when Bishop Thomas Lauder dedicated the building.

In the 1470s Bishop Lauder added the small porch on the south side and then began work on the lofty tower projecting from the NW corner. It bears his arms and those of his successor, Bishop Livingston, but was probably only completed c1500 by Bishop Brown, when a new square-headed window was inserted in the adjoining aisle. Other windows on the north side have quatrefoils in the heads, and one window uses this motif in reticulated tracery. The vaulted lower stage of the tower contains a Pictish slab and other old carved stones including an early 16th century incised slab depicting Al-exander Douglas, Rector of Moneydie. Unusual survivals here are the mural paintings, probably of c1520, depicting the Judgment of Solomon and a Woman taken in Adultery, reminding us it was used as a consistory court.

The west front of Dunkeld Cathedral

ECCLES PRIORY   Borders

Cistercian Nuns   NT 764413
By Eccles churchyard, 8km NE of Kelso

In the grounds of Eccles House, adjoining the kirkyard, is what is thought to be the south wall of the church of a Cistercian nunnery founded c1156 by Gospatrick, Earl of Dunbar and his wife Deirdre. The rere-arch of a former doorway is visible. Adjoining it are two vaulted cellars of the east range and a staircase leading up. The next room appears to have been a chapter house. A well may perhaps mark the site of a lavatorium in the cloister SW corner. Loose 12th and 13th century column capitals lie nearby in the gardens.

EDINBURGH FRIARY   Lothian   *Carmelite*   Location Uncertain

Little is known about a Carmelite friary founded by the Provost and Baillies of Edinburgh as late as 1526, so that the community may not have had time to erect a full layout of monastic buildings before being dispersed at the Reformation.

EDINBURGH FRIARY   Lothian   *Dominican*   NT 261735   South side of city centre

In 1230 Alexander II gave land now bounded by Cowgate and Drummond Street for the founding of this friary, which was badly damaged by the English attacks on Edinburgh in 1528 and 1544. It was finally wrecked by reformers in 1559. The land was handed over by the Crown to the magistrates and town council in 1566.

EDINBURGH FRIARY   Lothian   *Franciscan*   NT 256733   South side of city centre

This friary beside Candlemakers Row was established c1450 by six friars sent over from Holland in 1447. It also suffered from the English attacks in 1528 and 1544 and was closed in 1559. Following a petition from the town council in 1562 Queen Mary allowed the site to be used as a burial ground to relieve overcrowding at St Giles. The existing Greyfriars church on the site was built in 1602-20, although the western half used for over two centuries as a separate church dates from 1718, following an explosion of gunpowder stored in the original west tower.

ELCHO PRIORY   Perthshire   *Cistercian Nuns*   NO 141218   3km SE of Perth

A 1m high bank enclosing a court 35m square at Grange of Elcho on the south side of the River Tay marks the site of a Cistercian nunnery founded in the 13th century. It was burnt by the English in December 1547, and in 1559 a band of reformers from Perth drove out the nuns from the then probably mostly derelict buildings. The lands were made into a temporal lordship for Lord Scone in 1610. Excavations in 1983 found traces of the church and sherds of pottery and glass dating from the 14th century through to the 16th century. The church measured 8m by 21m and was heavily buttressed on the south side. It did not extend as far as the east range of the claustral buildings.

0 ⌞ ⌟ 5
metres

NAVE   CHOIR

Plan of the Franciscan friary church at Elgin

ELGIN FRIARY   Moray   *Dominican*   NJ 212629   At west end of city centre

This was the first Dominican house in Scotland, founded by Alexander II in 1234. Some slight remains of it were said to be still visible in 1887 in a field north of the castle, near the south bank of the River Lossie. Most of this area is now built over.

ELGIN FRIARY   Moray   *Franciscan*   NJ 219628   At east end of city centre

A Catholic convent school run by the Sisters of Mercy in Abbey Street lies on the site of a Franciscan friary founded c1281 close to the south side of the High Street. Greyfriars Street lies nearby. The convent buildings are said to stand on old foundations. On the north side is a chapel formed from the friary church supposedly built by Bishop John Innes in 1479, which was restored from ruin c1895-90 with the 3rd Marquess of Bute as patron. Original features include a sacrament house on the north side , a squint from a mural chamber set high up and five two-light windows on the north side. The town council took possession of the buildings c1559 and used part of them as a court house from 1563 onwards, thus ensuring their preservation to a later period than usual.

The west towers at Elgin Cathedral   *The tomb of Bishop Winchester in Elgin Cathedral*

ELGIN CATHEDRAL   Moray   *Secular Canons*   NJ 222631   NE end of city

The bishopric of Moray founded in 1107 was originally based at Birnie, an ancient Culdee monastic site. The fourth bishop, Richard (1187-1203) moved to Spynie, to the north of Elgin, where his successor Bricius Douglas founded a college of eight canons and later bishops developed a fine fortified palace. Footings of a wide rectangular church 22m long were once traceable there. In 1224 Bishop Andrew de Moravia with strong support from King Alexander II began the existing cathedral of the Holy Trinity just east of the medieval bounds of Elgin. The chapter or college of canons was increased to twenty three, including seven dignitaries, and there were 22 vicars choral, plus many chaplains. Following a fire in 1270 which also damaged some of the canons' houses, the original short and aisleless east end was replaced by the existing structure under Bishop Archibald (1253-98).

Bishop Alexander Bur (1362-97) fell out with King Robert II's second son Alexander Stewart, Earl of Buchan. In retribution for being excommunicated the earl descended on Elgin in June 1390 and burned the entire town, including the cathedral and all the houses in the precinct. Gradual rebuilding was delayed by a raid by Alexander Macdonald, son of the Lord of the Isles in 1402, but the work must have been completed by the 1460s when Bishop David Stewart was able to find funds for adding a huge tower to the palace at Spynie in response to threats by the Earl of Huntly. In January 1555 the cathedral was the scene of a battle between the Innes and Dunbar families, two of the latter being respectively Prior of Pluscarden and Dean of Moray. Both families had tombs of their ancestors in the cathedral transepts. The last mass within the cathedral was held in October 1594, in the presence of the rebel earls of Errol and Huntly after their recent victory over the royal forces. The building was already then becoming ruinous since it was never used for Protestant worship and since the 1540s Bishop Patrick Hepburn, d1575, had alienated church lands to members of his family, leaving it without endowments. In 1567 the Regent Moray ordered removal of the lead covering of the roofs. What remained of the choir roof timbers collapsed in 1637, the rood screen was torn down by Covenanters in 1640, and further damage is said to have been done by Cromwellian soldiers. The ruins were used as a quarry after the central tower collapsed in 1711, but this process was arrested in the 1820s, the ruins eventually becoming a monument in State care.

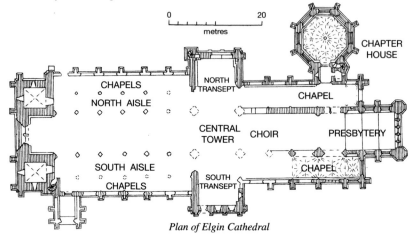

Plan of Elgin Cathedral

Looking down onto the east end and chapter house of Elgin Cathedral

Apart a few windows and tombs most of the remains of the cathedral date from c1224-98. With an external length of 80m it has a pair of 27m high western towers flanking the west bay of the nave, and a very fine double-portal doorway between them. The other six bays of the nave were double-aisled to allow a rows of outer chapels beyond the main aisles. The eastern part of the south side had this arrangement (which is unusual in Britain) by the 1250s and the rest was added after the fire of 1270. The westernmost bays contained doorways, with a porch on the south side. Little of all this now remains apart from the outer wall on the south side. Just pier bases remain of the arcades and of the central tower not a trace remains. Low walls remain of the north transept with its NW corner staircase turret, but the south transept stands high, with a tier of round-arched windows set over a pair of lancets and a vesica window over a SW doorway adorned with dog-tooth. Each transept has two tomb recesses in the end wall, one being that of Bishop James Stewart, d1460.

The eastern parts of c1270-1300 are better preserved and the east end of the presbytery is nearly complete, with niches in octagonal corner turrets and between them two tiers of five east lancets. The upper row corresponded to the clerestory windows over the arcades and above them lies a wheel-window, now without tracery. On the south side is a fine set of vaulted sedilia and on the north side are tombs of bishops Archibald and Pilmore. A few slabs of Tournai marble remain in the floor with indents of former brass memorials. The three eastern bays of the five bay St Mary's aisle on the south side still retain their vaults protecting the central tombs of the first Earl of Huntly and one of the Hays of Lochloy, whilst there are recesses with effigies of bishops Pilmore (1326-62) and Winchester (1436-60). One outer window here still retains four complete lights. Projecting from the St Columba's aisle on the north side is a lobby leading to the octagonal chapter house. This room, remodelled in the 15th century with a wall-bench, five canopied seats facing the doorway, and a fine vault with a clustered central pier, remained in use for meetings long after ruination of the rest of the cathedral. There are many fine carvings here and the shields on the capital of the central pier include the Five Wounds of Christ and the arms of Bishop Andrew Stewart (1482-1501)

FAILFORD FRIARY   Ayrshire   *Trinitarian*   Location Uncertain

By c1540 the lands of the Trinitarian friary established here c1240 by David de Bernham were in secular hands. Nothing else appears to be known about it.

FEARN ABBEY   Highland   *Premonstratensian*   NH 837773   7.5km SE of Tain

The community of Premonstratensian canons originally established near Edderton by Ferquhard, Earl of Ross in 1225 moved here c1238. The original buildings are said to have been of clay and rough stone. The existing church was begun c1340 and was given a stone roof by Abbot Finley c1408-36. Only thin low walls (refaced externally) remain of the large transeptal St Michael's aisle on the south side added by Abbot Finlay McFaed, d1485, whose arms appear on the top of the recess containing an effigy of a priest in the transept south wall. The dormitory beyond it also begun by Abbot McFaed was only completed by his successor, Abbot Thomas McCulloch. After the Reformation the church was used for parish worship with the east end closed off as the burial aisle of the Rosses of Balnagown. After the roof collapsed in 1742 material was taken from the west end of the nave and the dormitory to help build a new church, but in 1772 that building was abandoned and the abbey church then restored again.

Originally each of the six bays of the ashlar-faced church had two lancet windows between the dividing buttresses. Most of the northern lancets remain, although two are blocked, and five survive on the south, the western two small and placed high up to allow for a cloister walk below them. There are also four of equal height in the east wall. above them is an early 15th century window, now partly filled with a late 18th century Venetian window. The west wall cutting off the lost sixth bay and the belfry above it are of the 1770s. Opposite the blocked arch to the St Michael's aisle is another blocked arch, probably 17th century. It suggests a former chapel or burial aisle here, but the only one surviving on this side lies one bay further east. At the east end of the south wall is a small chapel, probably part of the work carried out after the church was described as ruinous and neglected in 1541. The church has quite a collection of 17th and 18th century monuments, including a huge tomb of Admiral Sir John Lockhart Ross, d1790.

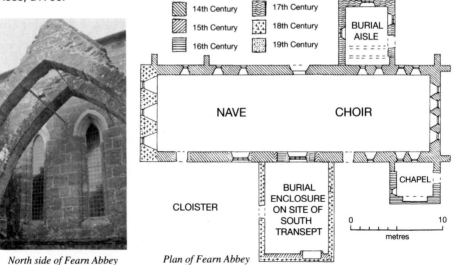

North side of Fearn Abbey   *Plan of Fearn Abbey*

The tomb of Abbot Finlay McFaed at Fearn Abbey

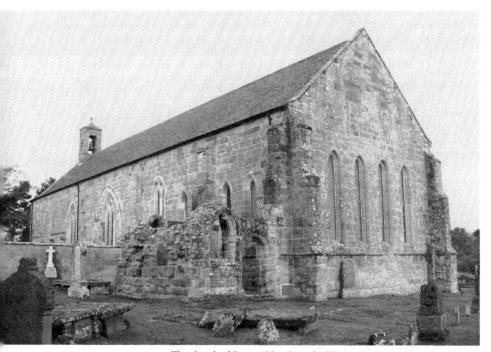

The church of Fearn Abbey from the SE

FORTROSE CATHEDRAL Highland *Secular Canons* NH 727565 E side, Black Isle

A see was established at Rosemarkie in the early 12th century, using as a cathedral a church of St Peter supposedly founded by St Boniface as part of a 7th century Celtic monastery. A new cathedral was built 2km to the SW after Bishop Robert was allowed by Pope Gregory IX in 1236 to reform and enlarge the cathedral chapter. Resistance by the Celtic priests may have prompted the change of site. The new settlement, now known as Fortrose, was long known as Chanonry (and the nearby point still is) from the houses of the canons originally grouped around the cathedral. At the Reformation the building was not required for parochial services and in 1572 William, Lord Ruthven was granted the lead from the roof. The nave and choir were dismantled to provide materials for building the Cromwellian fort at Inverness in the 1650s. The south aisle survived in use as a burial aisle for the Mackenzies of Seaforth and the sacristy was used for town council meetings. By the 1850s both parts had become officially regarded as ancient monuments and they are now maintained by Historic Scotland..

The south side of the nave has an aisle formed of two vaulted parts each with a two bay arcade with heads on the pier and faces on the hoodmould labels. The western part was more in the nature of a two bay aisle probably with an altar in a narrower eastern third bay with just a tomb recess facing the nave instead of a wide arch as in the other bays. The tiny vaulted chapel on the south side of this part was built c1635 by Alexander Mackenzie of Coul. On the south side are traces of a two storey porch. West of there the walling is rubble rather than ashlar and there is a small lancet, and, facing west, a window with Y-tracery. See photo on page 8.

The slightly earlier eastern part of the south aisle is wider and had a five-light east window with Geometrical tracery and a pair of four-light south windows with remains of intersecting tracery. At the SW corner is a square staircase turret broached into an octagon higher up. This grand building served as a chantry chapel built to accommodate the tomb of Euphemia, Countess of Ross, d1394. It bears the arms of her son Alexander Leslie, Earl of Ross, d1402, and those of John Bulloch, Bishop of Ross (1420-39). The tomb lies under an arch between it and the nave and has now only a fragment of an effigy. Euphemia's second husband was the notorious Alexander Stewart, Earl of Mar, whose own tomb lies in Dunkeld Cathedral. It was he who burned in 1390 both Pluscarden Priory and Elgin Cathedral. West of Euphemia's tomb is another arch over a canopied monument with the defaced effigy of Bishop Robert Cairncross, d1545. There are many 17th and 18th century memorials.

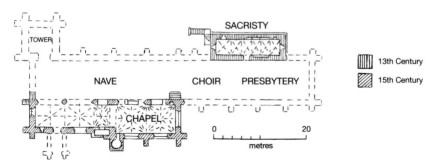

Plan of Fortrose Cathedral

The cathedral was 60m long internally, with a nave and choir each of five wide bays. Very slight traces remain of footings of the choir south wall and of a late medieval tower similar to that at Dunkeld but projecting north from the nave NW corner rather than to the west of it. Three bays of the choir were flanked on the north side by a sacristy which is original 13th century work vaulted in six bays of rather varying widths. The upper storey now reached by an external staircase was rebuilt in the 17th century and remodelled in the 18th century.

FYVIE PRIORY   Aberdeenshire

Tironensian   NJ 765378
11km SSE of Turriff

A rectangular mound of stones with a small cross on top is thought to mark the site of the church of a small priory which was colonised from Arbroath in 1285 with Reginald de Cheyne as patron. The priory was dissolved as early as c1508.

The south aisle of Fortrose Cathedral

The chapter house of Fortrose Cathedral from the SW

GLASGOW CATHEDRAL   *Secular Canons*   NS 602655   East of the old city

St Kentigern (also known as St Mungo) founded a monastery here in the late 6th century. It was ruled by an abbot-bishop until reorganised in the early 12th century. The new cathedral consecrated in 1136 seems to have been an aisleless cruciform building of modest size. Nothing remains of it and only one voussoir later used as rubble infill remains of the large aisled eastern extension built by Bishop Jocelyn and consecrated in 1197. The outer walls of the aisles remain of the new aisled nave probably completed by Bishop Walter (1207-32), but the arcades, notably narrower than those further east, are late 13th century. The next bishop, William de Bondington, chancellor to Alexander II, again rebuilt the east end as a two storey structure, with a shrine of St Kentigern behind the high altar on the upper level and the saint's tomb below, both levels being vaulted and containing numerous chapels to make up for the lack of any transeptal chapels. This work is assumed to have been completed by the 1270s, when materials were obtained for building a treasury on the north side and a new central tower. By the 1290s the central tower had been built, along with two unusually shallow transepts, neither of which projects beyond the outer walls of the aisles.

The main body of the cathedral has an external length of about 90m. The two storey chapter house projects further east and originally extra length was attained by a pair of western towers until they were removed in 1846. The NW tower once stood as high as the central tower and had buttresses only at the centre of each wall. The other tower additionally had corner buttresses and seems to have been a 15th century addition left unfinished at a level below that of the nave roof. The nave is rather plain work, eight bays long with a twin western doorway and another doorway on the south side in the third bay from the west where a shallow porch is formed between the buttresses. The timber roof is original late medieval work much restored. The doorway under the north transept was used by the canons and clergy, whose houses lay grouped on this side. The triforium and roof are reached by a staircase at the NE corner. An ogival-headed doorway off this staircase was inserted in the 15th century to give access to a rood loft across the east end of the nave and aisles which is first mentioned in 1458. By the time of the Reformation a series of altars stood against the west side of each nave pier, each having a reredos against the pier and low railings on the other three sides.

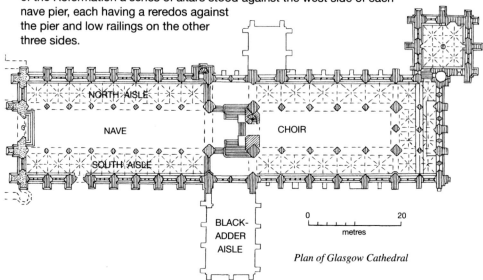

BLACK-
ADDER
AISLE

0   20
metres

Plan of Glasgow Cathedral

The eastern arm is about the same length as the western part but consists of a choir and presbytery of five bays plus an east end with four square chapels opening off an ambulatory. These chapels have pairs of lancets but the main aisles have three light windows, those of the choir aisles noticeably bigger than those of the nave aisles because of the greater bay width. In the vaulted lower level there are smaller intermediate piers between the main ones, and also intermediate buttresses with lancets on either side. Here lies an effigy thought to be of Bishop Wishart, d1316, and a 15th century slab by a West Highland mason depicting a priest, the only medieval monuments now remaining. The choir has a clerestory of lancets in triplets and a modern roof re-using 16th century ribs and bosses, whilst the aisles have ribvaults. In a remodelling during the 15th century the choir stalls were moved into the eastern arm from further west, a splendid pulpitum was inserted between the eastern crossing piers, and the high altar replaced St Kentigern's shrine.

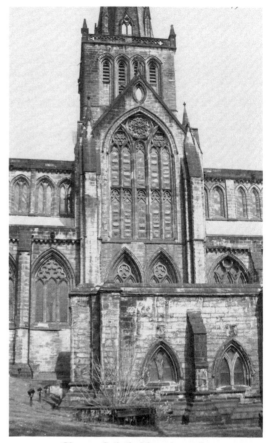

Glasgow Cathedral from the south

Each level of the chapter house has a ribvault with a central pier, these being insertions of the time of Bishop William Lauder (1408-25). The lower level has pairs of lancets and the upper level two-light windows and a fireplace. The intermediate buttresses project further than the corner ones. Although it bears the arms of Archbishop Robert Blackader (1483-1508) which also appear on the altar platforms in front of the pulpitum, the large new chapel two bays wide projecting southwards for four bays from the south transept may be of late 13th century origin. The upper level intended to take a shrine was never completed. On the northern side of the choir is the vaulted treasury, also late 13th century. Originally it had an upper level used as a sacristy.

Inside the Blackader Aisle at Glasgow

GLASGOW FRIARY   *Dominican*   NS 599651   East side of old city

Black Friars Street commemorates the former Dominican friary established c1246 some way south of the cathedral. Slezer's engraving of the building made in the 17th century suggests the friary church had a central tower later raised over a central passage between the nave and choir. Queen Mary gave the friary to the university and the church remained in use as a college chapel. It was rebuilt in 1699-1702 after a fire in 1660. The college moved elsewhere within the city in the 1870s and a railway station was then built on the site.

GLASGOW FRIARY   *Franciscan*   NS 598653   East side of old city

During work on the City Science Development in the High Street in 2003 slight traces of the SE corner of the Franciscan friary of St Mary founded in 1476 were revealed. Also found were a well and twenty skeletons which were later transferred to the present day Franciscan premises in Ballater Street. Local reformers began to demolish the friary in 1559, and the Duke of Chatelherault and the Earl of Argyll supervised completion of the destruction in 1560.

GLENLUCE ABBEY   Galloway   *Cistercian*   NX 185587   1.5km NW of Glenluce

In 1192 Roland, Lord of Galloway founded this abbey for Cistercian monks from Dundrennan. Little is known about the abbots or community during the medieval period. Robert Bruce was a visitor in 1329, and James IV stayed when on pilgrimage to Whithorn. By the 1540s custody of the abbey lands were being disputed by the Gordons of Lochinvar and the Kennedy earls of Cassilis. At one point the community lived at Maybole under protection of the Kennedys until the Gordons were dislodged from Glenluce after arbitration, but Commendator Thomas Hay and six monks are said to have been in residence at the abbey in 1572. The Gordons later regained the lands but they were later purchased by the Crown and annexed to the see of Galloway.

Only low walls mostly of c1200 with clasping corner buttresses remain of most of the church. The church had an aisled nave of six bays with arcades of octagonal piers (just one pier base remains), and three west doorways, an unusual arrangement in Scotland. There are transepts with pairs of rib-vaulted eastern chapels and a short presbytery. The south transept stands higher, this part having been domesticated with three upper floors linked by a spiral staircase in the 16th century, when a gallery was added over the chapels here, the southernmost of which has an original trefoil-headed piscina. The walls between the chapels were late medieval insertions. The monks' choir lay in the eastern two bays of the nave and in the 15th or 16th century the western four bays were divided off and put to other uses, the south aisle being divided off from the rest as a separate room.

Cloister alley arcade at Glenluce Abbey

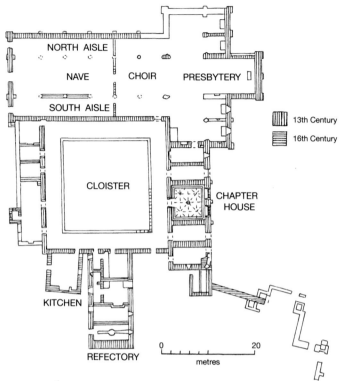

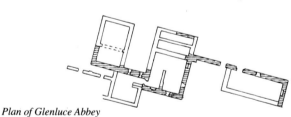

Plan of Glenluce Abbey

The eastern range was mostly rebuilt in the late 15th century and has a well preserved chapter house vaulted in two bays by two bays with foliage capitals on the central clustered pier and ceiling bosses with more foliage with the arms of Scotland and Galloway and rosettes with faces. This room has a west doorway with human heads on the hoodmould and a pair of rather short three-light east windows (see page 20), between which is a stall for the abbot with a trefoil head with a mitre flanked by rosettes. Between this room and the church are the usual sacristy and then a slype or passage, and to the south of it are a pair of barrel-vaulted rooms, and then a small reredorter. The dormitory above had a tiled floor. The adjoining alley of the cloister has been partly reconstructed. On the south side of the cloister, by the lavatorium or wash basin, is the refectory, set north-south and remodelled in the 16th century, when an upper storey was provided. The lower level was divided into two chambers, one with a fireplace and latrine, plus two other barrel-vaulted rooms, one of which seems to have been a brewhouse. West of here is a square kitchen with a south end fireplace. Most of the west range appears to be 16th century rebuilding. It includes two vaulted rooms and has a projecting west turret with a dovecot at the top. To the SE of the main buildings is are remains of another group of rooms, probably the infirmary.

HADDINGTON FRIARY   Lothian   *Franciscan*   NT 518738   At east end of town

In 1878 foundations of the Franciscan friary founded by 1242 were discovered during drainage works beside Holy Trinity Episcopal church dating from 12769-76. The friary was burnt by English invading forces in 1355 and 1544 and its lands were officially secularised in 1567. The church demolished in 1572 was a fine structure probably with a high central tower since it was referred to as "The Lamp of Lothian"

HADDINGTON PRIORY   Lothian   *Cistercian Nuns*   NT 521740   East of the town

In 1178 Cistercian nuns were established here in a priory of St Mary near the south side of the Tyne by Ada de Warenne, who had been given Haddington by her father-in-law David I. In 1503 Princess Margaret Tudor, daughter of Henry VII of England, stayed here on her way north to marry James IV of Scotland. Here in 1548 was signed a treaty between the Scots and the French against the English then currently invading the district. Still surviving is the late 12th century nave of what was either the nuns' church or possibly a chapel of St Martin set by the nunnery precinct gateway. The chancel arch with a hoodmould and plain imposts and the two south windows and one north window are all round-headed. The walls are pierced by a series of square holes. The doorways and buttresses are additions of a later period when a pointed vault was added.

HOLYROOD ABBEY   Lothian   *Augustinian*   NT 269740   East end of Edinburgh

The palace of Holyrood, still in use as an occasional royal residence, was developed by the Stewart kings on the site of the former guest apartments of the Augustinian abbey founded by David I in 1128. In the abbey church David II was buried in 1371. James II was born in the palace and crowned, married and buried in the church, whilst James III, James IV, James V were all married here. Queen Mary married Lord Darnley in the church in 1564, but her later marriage to the Earl of Bothwell was held in the more private palace chapel, the eastern parts of the church having been recently dismantled by order of the General Assembly of the Reformed Kirk. The church had twice been recently re-roofed as a result of the disastrous English raids in 1544 and 1547, when the lead roof-coverings were taken away as part of the plunder.

All that remains of the abbey is the nave of the church. It was used by a parish and continued to do so until James VII revived the Noble Order of the Thistle in 1687 and a new church for the parish of Canongate was then erected elsewhere so that the abbey nave could serve as the chapel of the order, with new altars for Catholic masses and stalls to accommodate the Knights of the Thistle. A Protestant mob tore out all the new furnishings in 1688 and the building soon became derelict. The north arcade and the upper vault complete with the clerestory collapsed in 1768.

The NW tower of the nave at Hollyrood Abbey

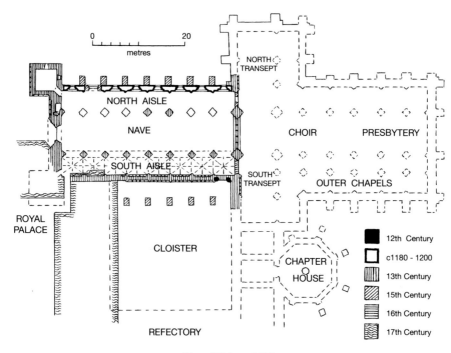

Plan of Holyrood Abbey

Part of the palace lies on the site of the west range, east of which lay the cloister. Little is known of the other domestic buildings except that the base of the central pier survives of the octagonal chapter house set beyond the east range. Bases also remain of flying buttresses at the outer corners. Of the original modest aisleless mid 12th century church there remains only a blocked south doorway, now within the south aisle of the surviving eight bay long nave, which was begun on the north side in the late 12th century where there is blind arcading with round arches. The south aisle wall with pointed-arched arcading and the arcades with their clustered piers and pointed arches and the west front were not built into the early 13th century after the older nave was cleared away. Partly now obscured by the palace, which has replaced one of its towers, this front has a deeply recessed central doorway, over which was a gallery. Unusually the towers projected from the corners rather than taking the place of the last bay of each aisle. The surviving NW tower has two-light upper windows over two tiers of blind arcading and appears rather short, its top being missing. The rib-vaults, of which only that in the south aisle now remains, were 15th century work. The buttresses added on both sides to support them bear the arms of Abbot Crawford, who also provided the existing north doorway. The supports on the south side are flying buttresses, allowing space for the northern cloister alley beneath them. The east window of 1633 lies on the site of the rood screen in the western arch of the crossing. The transepts have two bays of chapels beyond the aisles of the five bay long 13th century presbytery which once brought the external length to about 96m. In the later medieval period an outer aisle containing chapels was added on the south side of the eastern parts. See photo on page 6.

HOLYWOOD PRIORY Dumfries *Premonstratensian* NX 052713 4km NW Dumfries

One of the lords of Nithsdale founded this priory, which is first mentioned in 1255. A former manse now called Kirkland and the adjacent parish church of 1779 now stand on the site.

HOUSTON FRIARY Lothian *Trinitarian*   NT 052713   8km SE of Linlithgow

The advocate Sir Thomas Shairp's tall L-plan house of c1600 and its outbuildings in the parish of Uphall probably stand on the site of (and presumably incorporate re-used material from) a Trinitarian friary of the Holy Trinity founded in 1227 by John Graham, Lord Tarbolton.

INCHAFFRAY ABBEY Perthshire *Augustinian* NN 954225   16km west of Perth

On a low lying site once known as the Isle of Masses beside the Pow Water lies the overgrown site of an Augustinian abbey of St Mary and St John the Evangelist founded by Gilbert, Earl of Strathearn. His charter to it is dated 1200, but his son Gilbert was buried here in 1198 when Culdee priests may have still occupied what was an ancient monastic site. Originally a priory, it was made an abbey in the 1220s when Gilbert's son Robert was a generous benefactor. In the 1230s the possibility of moving the see of Dunblane here was considered but abandoned. Abbot Maurice blessed the Scottish army before its victory over the English at Bannockburn in 1314 and was later made Bishop of Dunblane. In 1495 the elderly abbot resigned and was replaced by Laurence, Lord Oliphant as the first of a series of lay commendators.

   Footings remain of the south wall of the church and in the 1890s this wall stood high enough to retain corbels for the north alley of the cloister, whilst there was a 13th century doorway into the 30m long west range which still survives as a result of being re-modelled as a house for James Drummond, who acquired the abbey lands in 1560 and later became Lord Madderty. The north gable of the range has four levels of windows and a chimney of c1600. Excavations have found traces of an early kitchen below this range and also showed that the north wall of the church was built over a bank which probably formed the northern side of the pre-Augustinian monastic enclosure. Traces were also found of the north transept and a sacristy not far east of it, plus parts of a substantial SW section of the precinct wall dating from the late 13th century and a 36m long building NW of the church which was probably a barn.

Inchcolm Abbey from the east

INCHCOLM ABBEY   Fife *Augustinian*   NT 189827   Island in Firth of Forth

Alexander I vowed to build a monastery on the island of Inchcolm after sheltering on it with a hermit when stranded by a storm in 1123. The hermit may have lived in the cell in the NW corner of the garden west of the church. The vault over the cell is much later. A charter of c1160 recording the handing over to the canons of property held in trust with Geoffrey, Bishop of Dunkeld, suggests that David I finally tried to honour his brother's vow in the 1140s but it took several more years after that to actually establish a priory on the island. The church erected during this period had just a small nave and tiny chancel. It was inadequate for a community of canons for whom a new choir had to be added c1200, and a tower was then built where the original chancel had been. The tower has a corbelled parapet and belfry windows of two lancets and a trefoil. Lower down it has a pulpitum formed of three narrow arches on the east side with foliage capitals and a rood screen on the west side, both of them partly obscured by later walling.

Further work began after the priory was raised to being an abbey in 1235. During that period it was favoured by the bishops of Dunkeld as their burial place, being regarded as a shrine of St Columba. A new east range was begun with an octagonal chapter house projecting from it, and the choir was lengthened and a small north transept built beside the tower. The chapter house has buttressed corners externally and the inside has a bench all round, with canopied seats for the abbot, prior and sub-prior, and a vault with a central boss carved with foliage. Above is a vaulted warming house with a fireplace on the north side added in the late 14th century. The chapter house doorway is round-arched and could be older work reset from elsewhere.

A new cloister begun at Inchcolm in the mid 13th century was left unfinished until gradually completed during the last two thirds of the 14th century. The cloister has thick inner walls with windows with seats in deep embrasures instead of open arcades. This is because the domestic buildings lie above the alleys, a layout commonly found in Ireland but otherwise rare in Scotland. This layout offered greater security in an age when the abbey found itself vulnerable to English raids, as in 1315, 1335, 1336 and 1385. The dormitory lies over the east alley and a refectory over the south alley, and guest rooms over the west alley, all three still having slab-roofs over upper vaults. The refectory has a reader's pulpit recess on the south side. The kitchen in the SW corner originally had an open central hearth but a fireplace was later made in its west wall. The original nave was eventually adapted to contain the abbot's hall with private chambers in the tower with the northern cloister alley below them. The former north transept was replaced by a smaller and more strongly built addition to provide the abbot with another room and help support the vaults then inserted in the tower.

Chapter House of Inchcolm Abbey

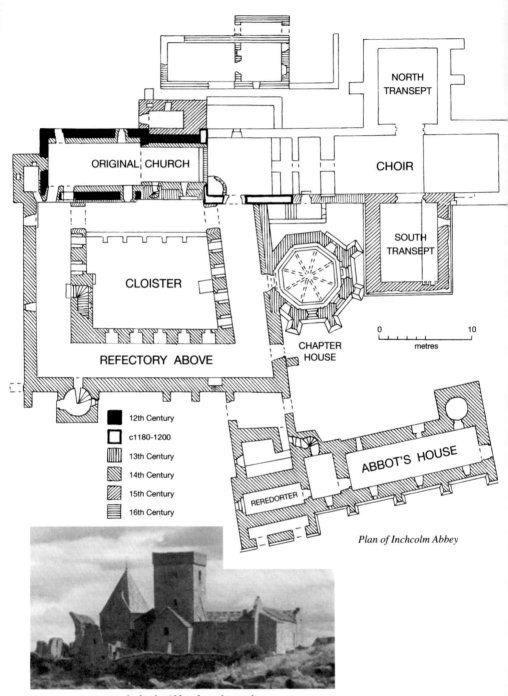

Plan of Inchcolm Abbey

Inchcolm Abbey from the north

The east range at Inchcolm from the cloister

Walter Bower, abbot at Inchcolm from 1418 until 1449 has found enduring fame as the author of the Scotichronicon, a history of Scotland covering the reigns from that of Malcolm Canmore to the time of James II. During his abbacy a new church was laid out beyond the original one, with transepts two bays long on either side of it. Unlike the rest this part was not required for domestic occupation after the Reformation and is reduced to footings apart from the south transept where the west wall has part of a pointed barrel vault. On the transept east side are traces of two altars with a piscina between them. Another piscina, trefoil-headed, lies in the south wall. West of the transepts is part of the choir of the 1260s with in its south wall part of a tomb recess with a group of clerics painted on the back. Here once lay the effigy of John de Leycester, Bishop of Dunkeld, d1266. Beside it is the new night stair from the dormitory added in the 15th century. The older choir of c1200 further west beside the tower became an open court and the chapel north of it was also abandoned, whilst the vaulted cloister alley through the base of the tower and former nave was closed off to form cellars and a new lean-to roofed north alley built against them. Another addition was a block to the east of the reredorter extending south beyond the dormitory. Possibly originally intended as an infirmary, the abbots may have transferred their residence to the upper rooms of this range.

Additions of the 16th century are the circular staircase turret at the tower SE corner and the staircase turret added near the west end of the south range of the cloister. James IV was a frequent visitor to Inchcolm and there were then usually about fifteen canons in residence. The abbey was pillaged and damaged by the English in 1542 and the canons had to live elsewhere when English forces garrisoned the island in 1547. Abbot Richard Abercromby was persuaded to resign in 1543 in favour of the teenage James Stewart, son the laird of Beith, who thus became commendator. He was present at the Parliament in August 1560 which reformed the Scottish church. The last few canons were allowed to stay at the abbey provided they abandoned Roman Catholic forms of worship. Two of them signed a document here as late as 1578.

INCHMAHOME PRIORY Stirlingshire *Augustinian*   NN 574005 Lake of Menteith

In 1238 Walter Comyn, 4th Earl of Menteith, established this island priory in the Lake of Menteith. Most of the 44m long priory church is 13th century work and comprises a nave and north aisle with an arcade of four bays (two survive) and a choir and presbytery of similar length with the lower parts of a sacristy on the north side. A NW tower four stages high was later inserted into the west bay of the aisle. The presbytery has on the south side a piscina and aumbry and a set of three sedilia below the stringcourse below the windows. The east window is a set of five lancets under an inner frame. (see page 20). The nave has a very irregular layout. The east and north parts of the church lie at an angle to the 21m square cloister to the south and its buildings which appear to represent a later campaign, along with a new south wall for the nave, which must originally been as wide at the east end as it is at the west. The nave west wall is clearly original work and has a fine doorway flanked by blind arcading with each spandrel of the arcading pierced by either a quatrefoil or a trefoil. Above was a three-light window.

Only the north and south alleys of the cloister were lean-to roofed structures, the other alleys being incorporated in the lower storeys of the west and east ranges. The west range was probably reserved for the prior and guests and has a spiral staircase at the south end. Little remains of the refectory on the south side apart from two doorways from the cloister. The west end was probably divided off as a kitchen. South of here is a fragment of the footings of the SW corner of an older refectory more in line with the north and east parts of the church. The east range continues further south to contain the warming house which has a double fireplace backed against a latrine projection. The day stair adjoins the refectory east wall and there was a night stair from the former dormitory at the north end. This stair lies beyond the chapter house, which has a stone bench all the way round inside, three east lancets and a barrel-vault. In later years this room served as a mausoleum for the earls of Menteith, whose ancestors had a castle on nearby Inchtulla. Monuments and old gravestones gathered here include the effigies of Earl Walter Stewart, c1295 and his wife, another knight of the Stewart family, and a low relief 14th century effigy of Sir John Drummond with images on either side of his head of St Michael killing a dragon and a bishop standing on a serpent. To the south of the chapter house is the slype or passage out to the canons' cemetery. See page 13.

The chapter house and remains of the east range at Inchmahome Priory

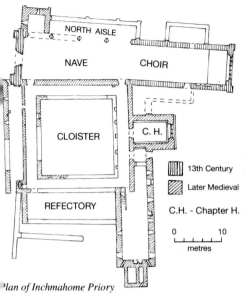

NORTH AISLE

NAVE CHOIR

CLOISTER C. H.

REFECTORY

|||| 13th Century

//// Later Medieval

C.H. - Chapter H.

0   10
metres

Plan of Inchmahome Priory

Inchmahome Priory

INVERBERVIE FRIARY   Aberdeenshire   *Carmelite*   NO 832727   NE of town

Large numbers of graves have been found where the friary lay close to the widening of the Berview Water known as Friars' Dubs near to the old bridge and mercat cross. David II is claimed as the founder and there is a unwitnessed and thus unreliabloe charter dated 1358. The friary was claimed to be "recently established" in 1443.

The west doorway of Inchmahome Priory

The guest house of Inverkeithing Friary

INVERKEITHING FRIARY   Fife   *Franciscan*   NT 129828   East of High Street

Still remaining beside High Street is the much altered guest house of a friary founded c1350. After the buildings were sold to John Swinton in 1559 the guest house was adapted as a house and most of the rest demolished, although some late 14th century cellars remain to the east of the public garden on the site of the cloister. A well survives near these cellars, and there is another next to the guest range, which in later years formed a tenement block. This part contained a hall over a vaulted kitchen and cellars and has had a pantiled roof since at least the 18th century. Most of the 14th and 17th century looking features, including several lancets, were renewed in a restoration of 1932-3. A pend giving access through to the cloister ran through the south end of the building, beyond which is a narrower 15th century extension. The block filling in the resulting re-entrant angle and the staircase turret now blocking the eastern arch of the pend are late 16th century. The northern end was once flanked by lower wings and has a doorway towards another range beyond, later replaced by a wider 17th century range demolished in 1932, leaving just the two successive roof raggles in the wall.

INVERNESS FRIARY   Highland   *Dominican*   NH 664456   North end of city centre

The graveyard in Friars Street is the site of a friary founded in the 1240s by Alexander II. A defaced effigy built into a boundary wall may depict Alexander, Earl of Mar, son of the notorious Wolf of Badenoch. Earl Alexander rebuilt the castle as his chief seat and was buried in the church here in 1435. Of that period is the octagonal pier (see page 10) which formed part of an arcade between the nave and an aisle, both of which appear to have been vaulted, as suggested by shafts on this, the only standing part of the friary.A papal indulgence was granted for the rebuilding of the church, which had probably been badly damaged during an attack on the town in 1428 by Alexander MacDonald, Lord of the Isles. Material from the site was taken off in the 1650s to build the large new Cromwellian fort. There are been some confusion between Blackfriars and Greyfriars here, but there is no certain evidence that Inverness ever had a Franciscan friary. The Dominican house here was the most northerly friary in the British Isles.

IONA ABBEY Argyll *Benedictine* NM 287245 On island at SW corner of Mull

Three very fine 8th century high crosses are the principal relics of the Celtic monastery founded by St Columba in the 6th century. There are traces of the ditch and ramparts of the enclosure to the NW, and a tiny 9th or 10th century oratory with antae known as St Columba's Shrine lies between the modern west range of the cloister and the clasping 15th century NW turret of the nave. Soon after arrival here c1200 Benedictine monks began a work on a cruciform church with an external length of about 35m. Of it there remain two low sections of walling on the north side of the nave (now connected by a long length of thin modern rebuild of 1908-10), the north transept with shallow altar recesses set either side of an image niche on the east side, and the adjoining part of the north side of the choir. Shafting suggests an intention to vault the transept. By the mid 13th century the east end had been lengthened by 14m but all that remains of that campaign is the eastern two thirds of the northern of two aisles then added to the choir, now forming a two storey sacristy with an upper arcade of two bays. Originally these arches were at choir level, but a crypt underneath the choir was removed and the floor levels dropped in the 15th century, when the doorway below the arches was inserted. By the end of the 13th century an ambitious scheme for a very long and wide new south transept with three vaulted east chapels had been begun and then abandoned.

In the 15th century the whole south side of the church complete with a new south transept and south choir aisle was rebuilt further out, widening the nave and choir from 5.2m to 6.8m internally and resulting in the central tower becoming a rectangle with a SW staircase turret instead of a square as originally. Also 15th century are the west end of the nave with its doorway, and the east end of the choir with a four light east window and three light side windows with Flamboyant tracery and a worn piscina. All the outer corners of the building have clasping buttresses. These works may have been with an intention for Iona to be a seat of a bishopric created out of the Scottish half of what was originally a Norse see of Sodor and Man once forming part of the province of Trondheim in Norway.

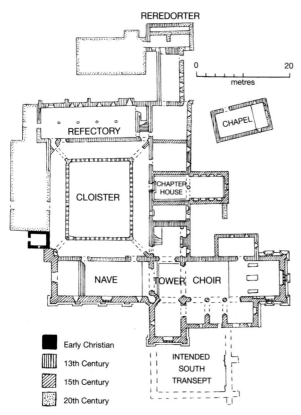

Plan of Iona Abbey

The south transept and choir both have wall-walks with corbelled parapets except on their gabled ends whilst the nave now has a wall-walk all around it. The choir aisle has a three bay arcade of arches with rolls and hollows and a pair of arches across its width connecting the piers with the outer wall. The circular piers have fine capitals carved with figures and creatures. All four arches under the tower are also 15th century, but an original 13th century arch survives at a higher level on the north side.

The effigies on the south and north sides of the presbytery floor of Iona Abbey probably depict Abbot Dominic (1421-c1425) and Abbot John MacKinnon (1467-c1498) respectively. Between them is a slab of Tournai marble with the outline of a brass figure of a knight, perhaps Lachlan MacLean, who added the huge tower house at Duart Castle in the 1370s. There is also a damaged slab showing a man in armour in the choir floor.

The abbey was abandoned after the Reformation but in 1635 the Bishop of the Isles had the choir restored for what turned out to be short-lived Episcopalian use. A plan to use the building as a parish church in the 1640s came to nothing. However by the late 18th century the romance of the place was being promoted by visiting antiquarians and in the 1874 the 8th Duke of Argyll had some repairs made. Further work was done on the church in 1902-4 and 1908-10. The Iona Community took over the buildings in 1938 and had mostly restored the cloister and its buildings by 1965. A new dormitory was built over what remained of the 13th century east range and a library was provided over the chapter houses added east of this range in the 15th century, when the original chapter house became a vestibule and was given a new round arched doorway from the cloister and a two bay arcade towards the new chapter house. East of here lies the detached and much restored early 13th century Michael Chapel.

North of the dormitory a passage connects it with the reredorter straddling a small stream (the reason for the cloister being north of the church). Adjoining the reredorter SW corner is the abbot's house which originally had an upper floor hall but now contains the laundry. To the NE of the reredorter lies the infirmary, where the doorway threshold alone predates 1964. The refectory originally had a reader's pulpit near the east end of the north wall and lies on the upper floor of the late 13th century north range. It is now reached by a stone stair to the dormitory from the cloister NE corner. Originally access was by a timber staircase from the blocked late 13th century doorway near the cloister NW corner. The cloister arcades are of 1959, based on 13th century fragments, but also retaining the layout of the heavier piers and arches at each corner inserted in the 15th century.

The church of Iona Abbey from the SW

IONA PRIORY   Argyll   *Augustinian Nuns*   NM 285241   Island at SW corner of Mull

This modest ruin is one of the best preserved medieval nunneries in the British Isles. Dating from soon after an assumed foundation c1200 are the church and the lower parts of an east (strictly speaking SE) range which contained the dormitory over thee rooms, the central one being marked out by its all-round wall bench as the chapter house. The slight off set in the east wall probably indicates the position of the south wall of the original tiny cloister. At the end of the 15th century the priory was provided with a larger new cloister 20m square with arcades of ogival-headed arches set on pairs of circular and octagonal columns, fragments of which are preserved elsewhere on the island. Little remains of the new west range of that period but there survives the refectory on the south, although its north wall has been rebuilt. This room has three narrow south windows, the middle one surmounted by what may be a very worn sheela-na-gig.

The church is just 19m long externally and was divided by a pointed arch into a nave which probably had the nuns' choir stalls in its eastern half and a square presbytery, the quadripartite ribbed vault of which collapsed in 1823. The doorway on the south side has a drawbar slot and the west gable has two round-arched lancets one above the other and recesses possibly for timbers of a former bellcote. Just one jamb remains of the pair of side by side east lancets. On the north side is a north aisle with the base of an outer doorway and an arcade of three round arches now blocked by later crosswalls in which are holes for timbers of a former west gallery. The circular piers have scalloped capitals but there are animals on the capitals of the responds. At the east end of the aisle an arch leads into a rib-vaulted chapel beside the presbytery. A stair mostly rebuilt in 1923 leads to a small room over the vault, also mostly now of 1923 and the chapel retains an east window, an aumbry on the south and a piscina on the north. See photo on page 23.

AISLE

0   10
metres

CHOIR

CLOISTER

CHAPTER HOUSE

REFECTORY

- ▦ c1200 - 25
- ▨ c1500
- ▓ Modern

Plan of Iona Nunnery

Iona Abbey before restoration

ISLE OF MAY PRIORY   Fife *Benedictine*   NT 668991   Island in Firth of Forth

Excavations revealed the full layout of this small priory for about ten monks (plus a few servants) founded by David I c1145. Set around a small court were a church 14m long with a west doorway, the earlier eastern range with a dormitory over a chapter house with a vault carried on two piers, the southern range with an upper floor refectory and the 13th century west range used to accommodate guests. St Andrews finally won a battle with Reading Abbey for possession during the Wars of Independence. Soon afterwards the community transferred to Pittenweem on the mainland, leaving just one priest to supervise the pilgrims arriving to see the shrine of St Adrian. Consequently the west range remained in use whilst the rest fell into ruin and after the island was granted to Patrick Learmouth of Dairsie in 1550 he added a round turret at the SW corner and created workshops in the church west end. One pilgrim buried here had set in his mouth a scallop shell, a symbol of St James of Santiago de Compostella.

JEDBURGH ABBEY   Borders *Augustinian*   NT 651204   On south side of town

Originally a priory founded c1138 by David I and Bishop John of Glasgow for Augustinian canons from St Quentin at Beauvais in France, and replacing an older monastery (from which fragments of an 8th or 9th century screen remain in the visitor centre), the community was raised to the status of an abbey c1154. By then work was well advanced on the eastern parts of the church and probably about to begin on the domestic buildings. The nave was begun in the 1180s and completed c1210 and the choir remodelled at the same time, probably because of structural instability on the sloping site since it was enlarged only very slightly from its original form. By the 1290s the buildings were all probably substantially complete.

The abbey suffered much from English attacks in the late medieval period, and needed frequent rebuilding. Excavations have shown that the abbot's house was ruinous by the mid 16th century when it and part of the east range were converted into makeshift artillery platforms and linked by a rampart to the surviving western sections of the precinct wall, which seems to have been furnished with towers back in the mid to late 14th century. By 1545 commendators of the Home family were in charge here and the estates of Jedburgh and Coldingham were made into a temporal lordship for them in 1606 and 1610. Parochial worship continued in the central part of the church but in the 1640s the tower threatened to collapse, and in 1668-71 a new parish church was created in the five west bays of the nave and north aisle. All traces of this work were removed in 1875 and the ruins then became an ancient monument, passing into state care in 1913. The then heavily buttressed northern crossing piers were stabilised soon after. The surviving lower parts of the walls of the domestic buildings were only partly exposed in the 1930s. Other parts were only laid bare in the 1980s.

The church is about 72m long and consists of an aisled nave nine bays long, a central tower with transepts, a choir flanked by two bay chapels, and an aisleless presbytery of three bays. The south transept was truncated in the 16th century and the cut-off southern part has footings of an east apse. The loss of both the transept south gable and the east gable of the presbytery makes the church slightly disturbing to look at. The north transept lost its apse during a rebuilding during which it was lengthened northwards with a four light end window and a pair of two-light west windows, the east wall being left solid. It bears the arms of William Turnbull, Bishop of Glasgow (1447-54). A crosswall dated 1681 on a tablet cuts off the northern part of the transept as a burial aisle of the Kerrs, whose descendants became marquesses of Lothian.

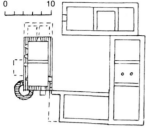

Plan of Isle of May Priory

The two bay arcades of the choir have tall circular piers rising through two levels with both arcade arch and gallery sub-arches under master arches, the piers having scalloped capitals and the upper arches having chevrons. Probably this design arose directly because of David I's choice of an English mason familiar with arcades of this type at the abbeys of Reading and Romsey. Stabilising the tower has required some rebuilding of the gallery level of the western bay. The original presbytery had an arcaded dado below the lowest of two rows of windows. What

The north elevation of the choir at Jedburgh Abbey

remains of the clerestory over the choir appears to be early 13th century work with one large lancet per bay. The south choir aisle vaulting boss has monograms of Jesus and Mary and the name of Abbot John Hall (1478-9), and the southern piers of the tower bear the arms of Abbot Thomas Cranston (1484-1501) and Archbishop Robert Blackadder (1483-1508). The archbishop's arms also appear on a tomb chest in the north transept and Cranston's arms also appear on the NW crossing pier. The upper parts of the tower arches were later blocked after being exposed to the outside by a lowering of the roofs in the 16th century. Above the arches each face had three lancets of equal height, except for a staircase disturbing the pattern on the SE.

In the nave the bays are wider than in the east end. Above the arcades of moulded pointed arches set on clustered piers with crocket and waterleaf capitals is a gallery on each side where each bay has two pointed arches divided by a slim pier under a round master arch. The clerestory above has four lancets per bay, the outer ones being blind and the inner two as windows. Waterleaf capitals here suggest a date of c1200-10. The west front has a magnificent doorway of six orders with chevrons and other motifs in the nave and nook-shafted round-arched windows in the nave. Above the doorway is a large round-arched window rising through both the gallery and clerestorey levels and then on top is a 15th century gable containing a twelve-petal rose window.

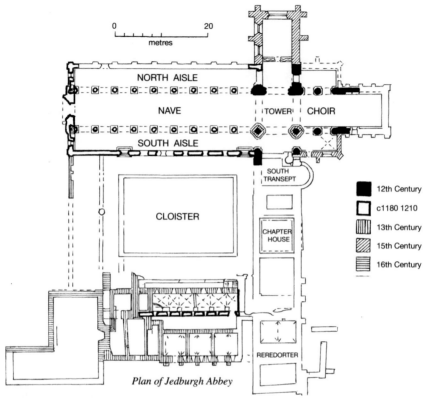

0 _____ 20
metres

NORTH AISLE

NAVE   TOWER   CHOIR

SOUTH AISLE

SOUTH
TRANSEPT

CLOISTER

CHAPTER
HOUSE

REREDORTER

■ 12th Century
□ c1180 1210
▥ 13th Century
▨ 15th Century
▤ 16th Century

Plan of Jedburgh Abbey

South arcade of the nave of Jedburgh Abbey

A stone bench all round marks out the square central room of the east range as the chapter house in its final late medieval phase. Earlier on it had projected eastwards from the range. At the south end were 13th century vaulted rooms extending down the slope towards the Jed Water on the edge of which was the reredorter. Originally the cloister was 25m square but it was later extended westwards and a new west range built further out of which little remains. On the south side a new alley was then made through the south range undercroft and the narrow remaining part in which are original round arched windows was provided with a ribbed vault. Above here was the refectory. Another block with rib-vaulted rooms further south, perched above the river bank, supported the abbot's rooms, although in the later medieval period the abbots transferred to the west range.

Lower part of south range at Jedburgh Abbey

JEDBURGH FRIARY   Borders   *Franciscan*   NT 650207   On west side of town

Observant Franciscans were established at Jedburgh by 1505 with Sir Andrew Ker of Ferniehurst being their main benefactor. Laid out in a garden since 1993 are footings revealed in excavations from 1983 to 1992 of a church 38m long aligned NW to SE and three ranges around a cloister 14m square on the NE side. The SE range had a square central room assumed to be a chapter house between a sacristy and the parlour and the NE range must have contained the refectory with a kitchen east of it. This range may be older than the rest and was perhaps an adaptation of a chapel which existed before the friars arrived. At the south corner were doors from the cloister into the church and the staircase up to the dormitory over the chapter house, and at the east corner was a lavatorium. Stone-lined conduits brought in water from the Skiprunning Burn and then others took away drainage from the cloister and its buildings. These tidy arrangements were disturbed by damage caused by the English invasion of 1523 after which it appears that for a while the friars had to use pits by the burn instead of the reredorter at the far end of their dormitory. The friary may have been left empty after other English attacks in 1544 and 1545. Evidence was found that the friars ate seafish rather than local freshwater fish and more meat than their rule allowed. Numerous apple and pear pips suggested possible cider production at the friary.

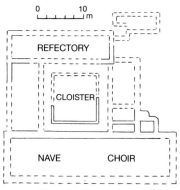

Plan of Jedburgh Friary

Last remnants of Jedburgh Friary

KELSO ABBEY   Borders   *Tironensian*   NT 730338   At south end of town

In 1113 Prince David settled Tironensian monks at Lindean near Selkirk. Four years after David became king in 1124 the monks moved to Kelso, probably to be near the important royal castle of Roxburgh. By 1152 the eastern parts of the church were complete enough for the king's son Henry, Earl of Northumberland to be buried there. Work on the nave clerestory continued through the late 12th century and the western tower may only have been completed shortly before the dedication (to St Mary and St John) by the bishop of St Andrews recorded in 1243. An interesting description of the abbey church dating from 1517 in the Vatican archives refers to it as having two pyramidal roofed towers corresponding to western and central transepts, upper roofs of wood covered in lead, a floor partly paved and partly bare earth, a screen dividing off the parochial nave from the monks' choir, and a total of twelve or thirteen altars. Only the western tower was then strong enough to contain bells and in times of peace there were said to be up to forty monks here under the abbot, prior and sub-prior.

Kelso was particularly vulnerable to raids from England and suffered on many occasions. After the Earl of Hertford's attack in 1545 the buildings were left without their lead roof coverings and even back in 1517 some of the cloister ranges were said to lack proper roofs because of English attacks. Some repairs were made by Commendator James Stewart but most of the internal fixtures and fittings of the church were removed by reformers in 1559. However it was not until 1587 that it was reported that the last of the monks living here had died out. The abbey estates were made into a temporal lordship for the future Earl of Roxburghe by James VI in 1607. A new parish church was created within the western transepts in 1648 and a stone vaulted gaol provided above it. A new church was built elsewhere in 1771-3 and the later insertions were removed before the ruin was taken into state care in 1919.

Kelso Abbey nave arcade

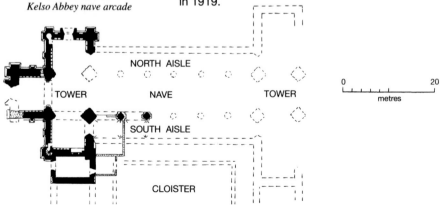

Plan of Kelso Abbey

Just one large, impressive and informative fragment still stands of the abbey buildings It comprises a pair of transepts set either side of a western tower with part of a galilee vestibule porch west of it, and two bays of the south arcade of the nave to the east. Adjoining the southern transept is a vaulted parlour which formed part of the lower storey of the west range. Nothing else is known about the cloister and its buildings but excavations in 1975 found part of what was thought to be the infirmary hall to the SE. It had bases of an arcade of alternate circular and octagonal piers between the main hall set from north to south and an aisle to the east of it, and one end of another building lay west of it. Also located by excavation were the SW pier of the central crossing tower in a position suggesting the nave was six bays long, and a possible corner of the main south transept, giving a length sufficient for two eastern chapels in addition to longer inner chapels or aisles beside the presbytery, which may have been apsed. The exact layout of the eastern arm of the church, however, is still unknown.

The north west transept at Kelso Abbey

The surviving part of the south arcade (see page 18) has two low circular piers with attached pilasters supporting two round arches. The slightly later triforium arcade above has a rhythm which ignores that of the arches below. It still uses round arches, as does the clerestorey and its wall passage above, but the remains of the south aisle vault with its keeled ribs show that pointed arches were used there. This vault was clearly not part of the original design. The main roof was never vaulted. The west transepts have intersecting arcading both inside and out and those walls not adjoining other structures have two lancets at levels corresponding to the main arcade, triforium and clerestory. There are rolls in the re-entrant angles between the pairs of external corner pilasters and at the top of each outer corner is a circular turret. The surviving NW corner of the west vestibule has an octagonal turret. The gables contained circular windows, that on the south being a 19th century rebuild and that on the north a later replacement of the original window slightly higher up. The transept west corners have spiral staircases to the galleries and roof. The surviving two sides of the west tower have quatrefoiled circular windows beside the transept roof-creases and belfry windows in the form of a row of three lancets of equal height, a very common arrangement in Scotland at all periods.

The north transept end wall contains a gable-headed projection containing a round-arched doorway of four orders adorned with nutmeg, billet and nailhead motifs on the arch and scallops or foliage on the capitals for the shafts, most of which are now missing. This was the main lay entrance to the parochial nave and has blind arcading above, behind which is a tiny mural chamber reached by steps down from the triforium passage. Only the north jamb remains of the even grander processional west doorway with five orders of shafts and an arch adorned with motifs such as chevrons, ringed rolls, cables and beakheads.

KILWINNING ABBEY   Ayrshire   *Tironensian*   NS 303403   In middle of town

Tironensian monks came over from Kelso some time in the 1160s or 70s to colonise this abbey dedicated to St Winning and St Mary, probably founded by Richard de Morville, Lord of Cunninghame and Constable of Scotland. The chapter house with its entrance facade of two-light windows either side of a doorway, all of them roll-moulded and round arched, probably dates from the 1180s, which is the likely period of the the lower parts of the south transept with one pointed arch and a clustered pier still remaining of the openings into two eastern chapels. The eastern parts remained in use as a parish church until 1775, and a later church stands on the site of the presbytery and north transept. Work on the upper parts and the aisled nave probably continued through the first third of the 13th century. Of that period remain the gable of the south transept with a vesica window over three tall lancets, the fine doorway once with three orders of colonettes and a dogtooth band between the south aisle and the NE corner of the cloister, and the arch which connected the south aisle with the southernmost of two west towers. The thick gable wall with a modest narrow west doorway to the north of this arch is later medieval and seems to represent a shortening of the nave by one bay down to seven bays. The NW tower was once the prison of Bessie Graham before being burnt as a stake as a witch in 1649. It was damaged by lightning in 1809 and then demolished and replaced by the existing detached structure.

Chapter House entrance facade at Kilwinning Abbey

In 1512 the earls of Angus and Glencairn forcibly entered the precinct and tried to force Abbot William Bunche to resign in favour of John Forman, Preceptor of Glasgow. There were 17 monks here in the 1540s, when the abbey still controlled 15 parish churches and the abbot had town houses in Irvine and Glasgow. In 1559 the Earl of Glencairn burned all the fixtures and fittings regarded as Popish and in 1562 he returned to deface some of the tombs in the church. In 1592 the lands controlled by the commendator were made into a free barony for one of the Melvilles, who in 1591 had tried to sue the Blairs for the return of all the abbey records which had been snatched away in 1571. The Melvilles sold the abbey and its properties in 1603 to Hugh, Earl of Glencairn, subsequent to which the buildings were quarried for their materials which were reused in such buildings as the dovecote and stables at the earl's main seat at Eglinton, and probably also his town house in the Seagate at Irvine. See photo on page 18.

South transept of Kilwinning Abbey

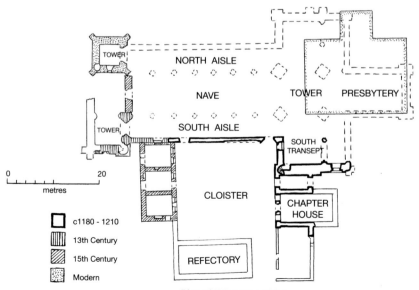

Plan of Kilwinning Abbey

KINLOSS ABBEY   Moray   *Cistercian*   NJ 065614   km NW of Forres

Cistercian monks were brought up from Melrose in 1150 at the behest of David I, who is said to have marked out the abbey precinct with his sword, the foundation supposedly being in gratitude for the king being guided out of wilderness by a white dove when he got lost when hunting. He is said to have spent the next summer supervising the construction of it. Within a graveyard which once served a later parish church a fairly recent wall encloses the south and west sides of the 29m square cloister. Footings here and there, two pier bases of the south arcade plus one on the north amidst later screen walls all hint at the layout of the 62m long church. It had an aisled nave of nine bays to contain both the lay brothers' and choir monks' stalls, a central tower and transepts each with two eastern chapels. The inner chapels were later absorbed into aisles running the full length of the three bays of the presbytery. The two rib-vaulted rooms still remaining were the SE chapel of the south transept and a later medieval eastern extension of the northern room of the east range. The southern end of this range with its reredorter was converted into a house with two lofty added turrets, one round and the other square, by Sir Edward Bruce of Clackmannan. He was created Lord Bruce of Kinloss after the abbey was suppressed c1560. His descendant the Earl of Elgin sold the property to the Brodies, who then sold most of the abbey stonework for the construction of the Cromwellian fort at Inverness in the 1650s.

KIRKCUDBRIGHT FRIARY

Galloway   *Franciscan*
NX 684511   NW side of town

Thomas Maclellan of Bombie and Grissel Maxwell's impressive house of the 1580s lies on the site of the garden of the friary founded c1455 and must have been built from the materials of the friary domestic buildings, which Thomas had obtained in 1569. A monument erected in the 1630s by their son with their effigies lies in the burial aisle they added on the south side of the friary church. The rest of the medieval church was replaced by a church of 1730, itself replaced by a school of c1840 which was adapted in 1919 back to form a modestly sized Episcopalian church (still called Greyfriars) which now uses the old burial aisle as a chancel.

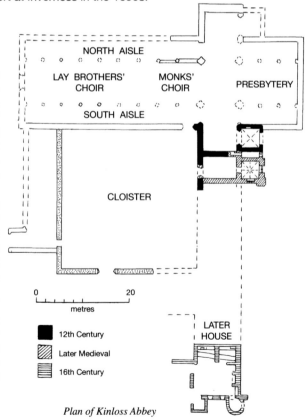

NORTH AISLE

LAY BROTHERS'
CHOIR

MONKS'
CHOIR

PRESBYTERY

SOUTH AISLE

CLOISTER

0   20

metres

■ 12th Century

▨ Later Medieval

☰ 16th Century

LATER
HOUSE

Plan of Kinloss Abbey

Kinloss Abbey

The interior of Kirkwall Cathedral   *Kirkwall Cathedral from the NW*

KIRKWALL CATHEDRAL Orkney *Secular Canons* HY 449111 In town centre

After obtaining control of Orkney in 1137 Earl Rognvald transferred the see from Birsay to a more central location at Kirkwall, where be began a new cathedral to house the relics of his saintly uncle, Magnus, killed on Egilsay in 1116. The cathedral appears to be the work of masons who had worked at Dunfermline and before that at Durham. It was a three-fifths scale version of the latter as completed c1130, cruciform with an apsed presbytery, although the choir aisles were probably always straight-ended. By 1153, when Earl Rognvald and Bishop William went on crusade, the eastern parts must have been roofed, most of the transepts completed, and parts of the outer walls of the nave aisles laid out, together with a pier on each side to help support a central tower. The positioning of doorways in the first and sixth days on the south side suggests that it was intended to build a cloister here and that the cathedral be served by regular canons.

There appears to have been a lull in building after Earl Rognvald's death in 1158, but in 1188 he was canonised and an energetic new bishop, Bjarne Kolbeinsson, was appointed. He seems to have brought in secular canons, who required a longer east end since their choir stalls would lie east of the crossing tower rather than under it. Three extra fully aisled bays of greater width than the older ones were added at the east end, rectangular chapels took the place of the intended apses east of the transepts, and work was continued on the west end of the nave, again with more widely spaced bays. It was also decided to provide high vaults, necessitating a hightening of the clerestory, but the aisles were completed lower than the original design of two full storeys. This phase was completed by c1250, but the belfry stage and spire of the central tower were only added in the early 14th century. The west front and the three west bays of the nave were only finally completed in a campaign of c1480-1510 using red sandstone ashlar contrasting with the 12th century red flagstone rubble of the aisle walls and the white ashlar used in the 13th century five eastern bays of the clerestory. The arms of Bishop Robert Painter (1477-1506) appear on a gablet over the main west doorway.

From the 1560s onwards only the choir and presbytery were used for worship, being closed off by wooden screens and filled with galleries in the 1630s. The nave remained roofed and in use for burials. When the spire was struck by lightning in 1671 it was replaced by a lower pyramidal roof. The post-reformation furnishings were removed in a restoration of 1847-50 sponsored by the Government, which then believed itself to own the building. A new spire was provided during a further restoration of 1913-30 when the interior of the building was reunified. No medieval memorials now remain.

The cathedral 69m long externally, with an eight bay long nave just 5.2m wide between round-arched arcades with circular piers. The west front is not very grand apart from three 13th century doorways with stiffleaf foliage on the capitals. The aisle doorways are of three orders with dogtooth and nailhead on the north and dogtooth and chevrons on the south. Contrasting red and white stone is used on alternate orders on the north and on alternating voussoirs on the south. The main doorway has as many as seven orders. The four-light window above with a transom is of c1500. The aisles have round-arched windows with hoodmoulds on shafts and a stringcourse linking their sills. On the north side the shafts have mid 12th century cushion capitals as far west as the east jamb of the fourth window and the sixth bay has a gabled 13th century doorway intended as the main laymen's entrance. On the south side heavier buttresses were added in the 15th century to the original pilaster strips. In the nave the clerestory windows are all small lancets, linked a stringcourse which rises over each one as a hoodmould, but the three west bays of the choir have round-arched windows of the 1140s.

Only the east jamb remains of the south aisle east doorway blocked up in the 13th century, whilst the sixth bay has a doorway replaced by Bishop Reid in the 16th century. The north aisle outer wall is topped by 13th century corbelling with trefoil pendants. The transepts have corner staircases and three levels of windows, the lower ones mid 12th century, but those of the top level closest to the tower having waterleaf capitals on the shafts suggesting a date c1200-20. Also of that date are the south transept doorway of four orders with dog-tooth and red and white stones set chequerwise and the tall point-ed crossing arches with chev-rons and waterleaf capitals. The presbytery of the 1190s is of yel-low rubble with pointed windows set at a higher level than the older ones further west and octagonal pinnacles over clasping corner buttresses. The presbytery south aisle has an ashlar SW bay with a window of two pointed lights un-der a round arch set over a door-way with nook-shafts and foliage on the hoodmould label. The east wheel-window set over paired sub-arches was restored c1840.

LANARK FRIARY   Strathclyde

Franciscan   NS 880437   S of town centre

A tablet on the side of the Clydesdale Hotel records that it stands on the site bounded by Broomgate and Castlebank of a Franciscan friary founded c1325-9 by Robert I. Here in 1418 died the dispirited friar Robert Hard-ing from England shortly after being rebuffed by the university students at St Andrews for trying to maintain support for the Avignon Pope Benedict XIII. Building materials from the friary were being removed without au-thorisation in 1566, although Sir Andrew Al-len had been buried in the church as recently as 1552. The site was then leased to James Lockhart of Lee but in 1580 was transferred to Bernard Lindsay.

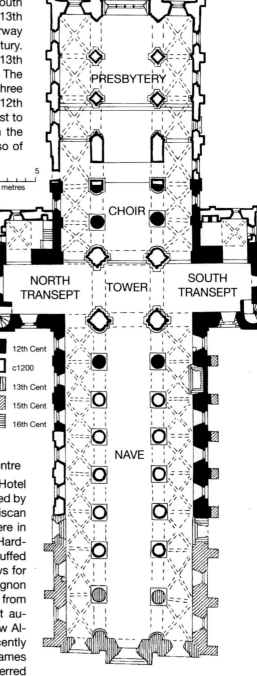

0   5
metres

PRESBYTERY

CHOIR

NORTH TRANSEPT

TOWER

SOUTH TRANSEPT

NAVE

■ 12th Cent
□ c1200
▤ 13th Cent
▨ 15th Cent
▤ 16th Cent

Plan of Kirkwall Cathedral

LESMAHAGOW ABBEY Lanarkshire *Tironensian* NS 814399   7km SW of Lanark

In 1144 David I had Tironensian monks sent over from Kelso to found this abbey, which was dedicated to St Mary and St Machutus and also enjoyed support from John, Bishop of Glasgow. It appears there was already a chapel on the site. Features exposed by excavations included a T-junction on a water supply pipe of lead, evidence of temporary buildings used while the abbey was under construction, confirmation that the cloister garth had always been a garden and burials in the east alley of the cloister near the chapter house entrance. After the abbey was damaged by the English in 1335 a passage between the cloister and an outer court to the south was created at the west end of the refectory. Near here excavators found a lavatorium of ashlar. The south wall of this block was rebuilt c1500 with heavy buttresses, and a new refectory created on an additional upper storey set over a vaulted cellar. With the exception of the west range the buildings seem to have been neglected by the mid 16th century, with signs of squatter occupation. Robert Ker of Cessford was granted the lands in 1602, and they passed to James, Marquess of Hamilton in 1623, but at least part of the church remained in parochial use until replaced by the existing building in 1803.

Lindores Abbey

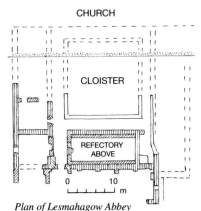

Plan of Lesmahagow Abbey

Remains of the refectory undercroft at Lesmahagow Abbey

LINCLUDEN PRIORY Dumfries *Benedictine Nuns*   NX 966779 N of Dumfries

The 15th century collegiate church (see the companion volume Medieval Churches of Scotland) lies on the site of a house of Benedictine nuns founded c1160, probably by Fergus, son of Fergus, Lord of Galloway. Following a request by the Earl of Douglas in 1389, the Pope allowed the priory to be suppressed by the Bishop of Glasgow and for the new college to take over its site and possessions.

LINDORES ABBEY Fife *Tironensian*   NO 244185   Just east of Newburgh

David, Earl of Huntingdon, son of King William, founded this abbey c1190 for Tironensian monks from Kelso, perhaps as a burial place for two of his children, who may have been buried in the small stone coffins in the choir floor. Guido, the first abbot, is said to have "built the place from the foundations" before his death in 1219 and the fragmentary ruins appear to be mostly of that period. The long nave had a south wall with blind arcading on both sides. Hardly anything remains of the north aisle probably added slightly later, or of the heavily buttressed NW tower, which was certainly later. The three bay long presbytery was also heavily buttressed, suggesting an intended vault. The transepts each had an eastern aisle divided by screens into three chapels. The east range has a vaulted passage next to the south transept and then the chapter house, now featureless. The day stair to the dormitory cuts into the NW corner of the larger room beyond. Another room to the east of it must be later. Only footings of the north wall remain of the refectory. Enough of the west range survives to show the lower storey was divided into six rooms. Fragments of other buildings remain further south, and a vaulted room in the garden of a cottage. Lengths of the precinct wall remain, with a gateway, and one wall of a possible 13th century barn.

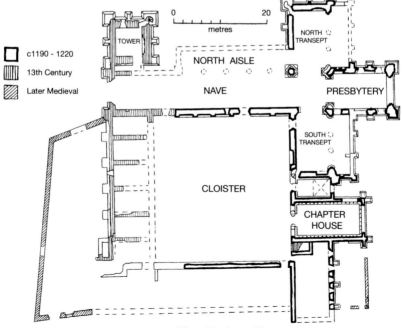

Plan of Lindores Abbey

LINLITHGOW FRIARY Lothian *Carmelite* NT 002771 south side of the town

In 1401 Carmelite friars took over an older chapel 21m long by 9m wide externally which they used as the nave of their church, adding a 16m long choir to the east reached by just a doorway surmounted by a wooden screen where the east wall of the original chapel had been. Excavations revealed footings of the friary buildings and found platforms for altars at the nave east end, and sockets for the posts of a retable or reredos behind the high altar in the choir. A chapel or other room was added to the west end of the nave by c1430. Beyond it lies a latrine which formed part of the house of the priest before the friars arrived and remained in use. The friars are thought to have obtained water from the Friars' Well in Rosemount Park.

Built upon older graves in the late 15th century was an east range 17.5m long and 7m wide containing a stair next to the church, then a sacristy, followed by a chapter house with evidence of a sprung floor, and a parlour, with a dormitory above all of these. The more slightly built south range added slightly later contained a kitchen, the refectory and another room at the east end. Not much of the west range was uncovered. To the east of the east range was found traces of a temporary building to accommodate either the friars or the masons and construction workers. The cloister

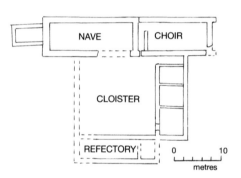

seems never to have been completed probably because of a lack of patronage by the early 16th century. Reformers destroyed the buildings in 1559 although the last few friars seem to have continued to inhabit the site for a while afterwards. Remains of stained glass windows broken in 1559 were found at each end of the church.

Plan of Linlithgow Friary

Lismore Cathedral

LISMORE CATHEDRAL Argyll *Secular Canons* NM 861435 13km N of Oban

A new bishopric of Aygyll was created in the early 13th century by dividing off parts of the rather scattered diocese of Dunkeld at the request its bishop, John le Scot, who precured the appointment of his chaplain Harald as the first bishop of Argyll. Possibly Iona was intended as the see but by the late 13th century the bishops had a new cathedral under construction at a site long associated with the 6th century Irish saint Moluag towards the northern end of the island of Lismore beside Loch Linnhe. Curiously, their residence in the form of a modest courtyard castle, also late 13th century work, lay as far as 7km away to the SW on a rather exposed site at Achadun. The nave added in the 14th century was probably complete by 1411 when there was an appeal to the Pope for funds for repairs and furnishings. There were frequent calls for the cathedral of Argyll and its bishop to be located on the mainland, but they had no seat there until Bishop David Hamilton built a tower at Saddel in 1508-10 after the lands of a dissolved Cistercian abbey were made into a barony. A later bshop, Neil Campbell, already possessed a castellated house at Kilmartin before his appointment in 1580.

Only meagre footings remain of the nave and a later medieval west tower, which were abandoned after the Reformation. The tower may never have been completed. The cathedral additionally was the parish church of Lismore and the choir has continued to serve this function. It was described as roofless in 1679, but was remodelled in 1749 when a new west gable with a birdcage belfry was built over what remained of the pulpitum between the choir and nave. New round-arched windows were inserted on the south side and a lower new roof provided which truncated the buttresses. The seating was arranged to face a pulpit on the south side until re-arranged in 1900, when the north windows were inserted and the east porch added. Original medieval features are the north and south doorways near the west end, the piscina and three round-arched sedilia in the south wall, and a doorway through to where there was once a NE chapel or vestry with an aumbry surviving in the main north wall.

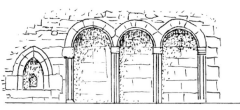

There fine graveslabs of the Iona type of the 14th to 15th century, two of them with tau-headed staves, lie within the church and outside are several other slabs from the 14th century to the 16th century plus a early 16th century tomb-chest lid.

Sedilia and piscina at Lismore Cathedral

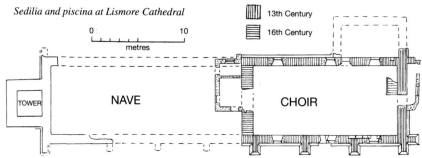

0 — 10
metres

▥ 13th Century
▤ 16th Century

TOWER NAVE CHOIR

Plan of Lismore Cathedral

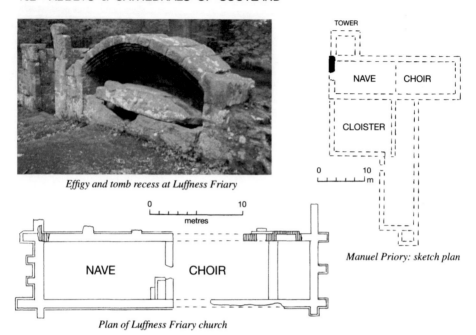

Effigy and tomb recess at Luffness Friary

Manuel Priory: sketch plan

Plan of Luffness Friary church

LUFFNESS FRIARY   Lothian   *Carmelite*   NT 471802   1km ENE of Aberlady

The friary is first mentioned in 1336 but the footings of the church 31m long by 8m wide externally which still remain in the grounds of Luffness House must go back to the late 13th century since there is a tomb recess in the choir north wall containing an effigy of a knight of that period. Just west of it is a doorway which led to a sacristy. Just a doorway in a cross-wall connected a nave with three west lancets and the choir with two east lancets, this arrangement of windows being suggested by the arrangement of the buttressing, the corners being angle-buttressed. A tomb slab of c1500 to Kentigern Hepburn still remains in the choir floor.

MANUEL PRIORY   Falkirk   *Cistercian Nuns*   NT 971764   3km W of Linlithgow

All that remains of the late 12th century church of a nunnery founded c1160 by Malcolm IV is the northern half of the west wall of the church, which was depicted c1739 by Cardonnel as a simple rectangle. It lies in a field to the west of the River Avon which is said to have washed away in 1783 the south portion of the site where the cloister and east dormitory range lay. An old plan indicates that the east alley of the cloister lay within the lower storey of the dormitory range. A drawing by Cardonnell suggests the church remained almost complete until 1739, but a record of John Colquhoun requesting permission to remove stone in 1741 suggests the buildings did not last much longer. The surviving outer NW corner projects out as a sloping buttress, probably a modern rebuild as a tower is said to have stood north of the nave here. One jamb of a Norman round-headed west doorway remains with the base of a nook shaft, and above are one and a half of a row of three lancet windows, plus a segment of a circular window in the gable. The corbels over the doorway supported the roof beams of a porch. There were still a prioress and four nuns here in 1552.

MARYCULTER   PRECEPTORY   Aberdeen

Knights Templar   NO 844999   SW of Aberdeen

By the River Dee about 11km SW of Aberdeen a burial ground contains low walls of a 13th century chapel of St Mary which served a preceptory of the Knights Templar. The foundation is usually credited to Walter Bisset of Aboyne c1221-36, although the knights may have obtained lands here from King William in the 1170s. A piscina or holy water stoup is the only remaining ancient feature of the 23m long by 7m wide building, which remained in use as a parish church until a new church 1km to the south was opened in 1782. Nearby Maryculter House, now the Deeside Hotel appears to have been built in the 17th century from materials from the preceptory. It was extended to the west after a fire in 1720, and in the 19th century to the north. After the fall of the Templars in 1312 the preceptory remained in use by Knights Hospitaller until the 1560s. A plaque over the cemetery gateway commemorates their connection with Maryculter. Good effigies of of the 1540s showing Gilbert Menzies with the Hospitaller cross at his throat, and his wife Marjory Chalmers from the church here now lie in the church of St Nicholas at Aberdeen.

The last remains of Manuel Priory

Melrose Abbey from the air

MELROSE ABBEY   Borders   *Cistercian*   NT 548341   On east edge of Melrose

A ditch across the neck of a promontory in a loop of the River Tweed 4km to the east of the abbey is the site of the monastery of Old Melrose founded according to Bede by St Aidan c635-51 where St Cuthbert later lived until 664, when he was made Prior of Lindisfarne. The monastery survived being burned by Kenneth MacAlpine in the mid-9th century and there appears to have been a big church there during the reign of David I.

In 1136 King David brought over monks from Rievaulx to form Scotland's first Cistercian abbey at Melrose. The Melrose Chronicle records its early history up until 1266. The king gave the abbey more estates in 1143 and the church was dedicated to St Mary in July 1146. Over the next hundred years several of the abbots were promoted to bishoprics, notably Jocelyn to Glasgow. He died and was buried here in the 1190s, and in 1249 King Alexander II's body was brought for burial here. The abbey became Scotland's greatest exporter of wool, much of it going to Flanders. The abbey lands seem to have suffered in the English invasion of 1314, and in 1326 King Robert Bruce assembled a rich package of gifts towards repairs at Melrose, which had been wrecked by Edward II of England's retreating troops in 1322. The church was again wrecked during Richard II's invasion of Scotland in 1385, although the English king did reduce customs dues on the abbey's goods to help pay for rebuilding it. The work continued for much of the 15th century but the new nave was never completed.

In 1545 an English force under Sir Ralph Evers desecrated the abbey church and damaged the tombs of the Douglas family. This prompted the Earl of Angus to join the Regent's forces in defeating killing Evers at Ancrum Moor, the English knight then being buried in the abbey church that he had ransacked. This prompted a raid by the Earl of Hertford in which was the abbey was burned. Back in 1541 Abbot Andrew Durie had been forced to resign in favour of a new commendator, who was James V's eldest illegitimate son James Stewart. He failed to provide funds for rebuilding, despite the protests of the monks, who also complained that the commendator had refused to admit any new brethren to maintain the number of sixteen required for services. Documents of 1534 and 1539 record the numbers of monks having already dropped from thirty four to twenty two and by the 1550s they were down to a dozen, whilst there were ten in 1565. There were complaints of lead from the cloister roof being taken away by local laymen in 1558, and of the church being further damaged in 1573 by Sir Walter Scott of Branxholm. The last commendator was William Douglas, Earl of Morton, executed in 1581 for past crimes, after which the abbey estates were divided up by the king.

The church seen from across the site of the cloister at Melrose Abbey

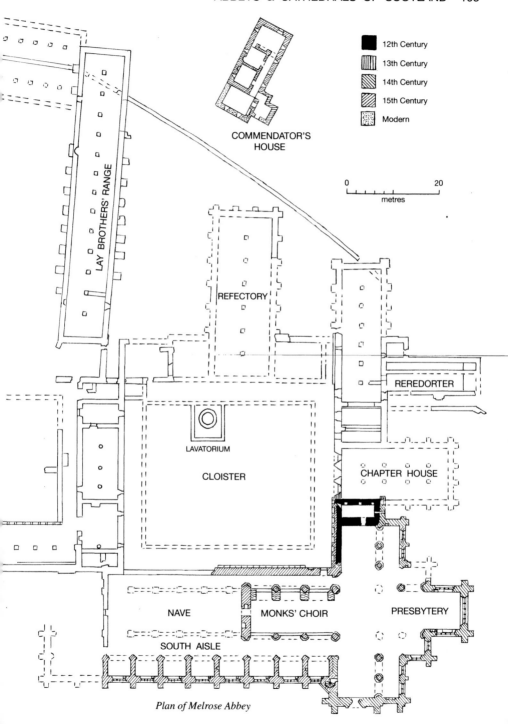

COMMENDATOR'S
HOUSE

12th Century
13th Century
14th Century
15th Century
Modern

0   20
metres

LAY BROTHERS' RANGE

REFECTORY

REREDORTER

LAVATORIUM

CLOISTER

CHAPTER HOUSE

NAVE

MONKS' CHOIR

PRESBYTERY

SOUTH AISLE

Plan of Melrose Abbey

The east end of the church at Melrose Abbey

Of the 12th century abbey church with a fully aisled nave eight bays long there remains only the base of its west wall, although excavations have shown that it had transepts as long but narrower than the present ones with three chapels each, the inner ones extending further east to flank the second of the three narrow bays of the presbytery. In the late 12th century a galilee porch two bays deep but unusually not extending the full width of the aisles was built at the west end. For drainage reasons the cloister lay on the north side of the church. Originally there was a lane between it and the lay brothers' refectory in the west range, now only represented by foundations, but a new west alley of the cloister later replaced the lane. The northern part of the west range was out of line with the southern part (west of which was a second cloister) and extended 105m from the church to a great drain serving the latrines. The original monks' refectory in the north range ran east west but a much larger new north-south refectory was built in the 13th century over an undercroft divided by piers into seven bays by two. South of it the base of a lavatorium projects into the cloister garth. Of the east range there remains a vaulted 12th century sacristy beside the transept. The chapter house beyond was rebuilt c1240 as a spacious chamber divided by piers into five bays by three. Parts of its entrance facade with windows on either side of the door-way still remain. The range continued northwards for another nine bays, and projecting east from the third and fourth of these bays was the reredorter, with a latrine pit on the north side. To the NE are traces of the abbots' hall and north of the refectory (now across a road from the main site) is the commendator's house, now essentially of the 1590s and later and serving as a museum, but probably of late medieval origin.

The first phase c1385-1400 of the new church may have been the work of an English mason from East Yorkshire. Of this period are most of the presbytery and south transept with their magnificent end gables, the east part of the north transept and three bays of the monks' choir in the nave up to the level of the top of the arcades. The massive rectangular piers carrying a surviving pointed barrel vault over these three bays of the nave date from the 1630s, when this part was adapted to serve as a parish church. The vaulting with ribs and bosses surviving over the presbytery east bay is original. The windows here are tall and have transoms and rectilinear tracery, the five light east window being without a parallel in Scotland. There is blank panelling over the window into the gable and the corner buttresses have canopied niches.

A second phase of c1410-20 in a style not at all then in vogue in England seems to be associated with two inscriptions on the inside of the south transept west wall. These refer to the mason John Morow from Paris as having also worked at Glasgow, Paisley, St Andrews and Whithorn, as well as on the collegiate church at Lincluden. The flowing tracery of the south transept five-light window and the fine doorway below it with a crouching figure of St John the Baptist at the apex of the hoodmould are assumed to be his designs, as must also be the round-headed doorways from the north aisle to the cloister and the north transept to the dormitory and the sacristy. He also must have begun the row of added chapels beyond the nave south aisle, but probably only the first one was completed with vaulting during his time.

A third phase probably nearly coincides with the abbacy of Andrew Hunter (1444-71), Treasurer under James II. Hunter's arms appear on the south transept vault and on a buttress between the fifth and sixth of the nave chapels. Of this period are the paired single-light windows in the north transept west wall and the clerestory of the monks' choir in the nave, plus the tierceron vaults of the transepts. Another vault of this type was intended to go over the monks' choir. West of here the new nave was never completed for its intended total of ten bays and part of the 12th century nave may have still stood in the 1560s. More of the south chapels were completed since a buttress west of the eighth chapel has the royal arms and the date 1505, and the west wall still stands of a central tower with tourelles upon shafts and a balustrade of square quatrefoils.

MONTROSE FRIARY   Angus

Dominican   NO 717593   N of town

This friary dedicated to St Mary was founded by Alan Durward in the mid 13th century but was abandoned in the 14th century and seems to have remained derelict until 1517, when it was refounded by the Earl of Albany on behalf of the young James V. The prior, sub-prior and eight other friars then installed were given custody of the hospital of St Mary in the town. The community was ejected by a party of reformers in 1559. The exact location of it remains uncertain.

Arcade in the cloister at Melrose Abbey

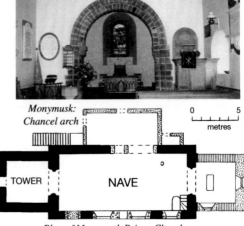

Monymusk Priory Church   *Plan of Monymusk Priory Church*

MONYMUSK PRIORY   Aberdeen   *Augustinian*   NO 685153   10km SW of Inverurie

In 1211 the bishop of St Andrews took objection to the Culdees here, relics of the old Celtic church, referring to themselves canons regular. A papal commission considered that they might have a dormitory, refectory and an oratory with burial right in the parish cemetery but they were not to be allowed to call consider themselves monks or canons without episcopal consent. A papal bull of 1245 was however addressed to the "prior and convent of the order of St Augustine" at Monymusk so the matter had been settled by then. It was probably about that time that a long new chancel was added to the parish church for the canons to use. The domestic buildings near the church were burned in 1554 as a result of negligence by the last prior, John Elphinstone, who was later hanged for various crimes and in 1587 material from them was taken to build Monymusk House. The existing short chancel is mostly of 1890 and burial enclosures have replaced the rest, but the chancel arch is original late 12th century work and so are the nave and west tower and the arch between them. The tower was reduced in height in 1822 and given a spire which lasted only until 1891. The nave has a set of large new Georgian windows on the south side and a 19th century north aisle.

NEWBATTLE ABBEY   Lothian   *Cistercian*   NT 333660   1km south of Dalkeith

Cistercian monks from Melrose came over to colonise this abbey founded by David I in 1140. Four pier bases found by excavations on the site of the lay brothers' western range and now lying loose in the grounds suggest work was underway on permanent buildings by 1160. One is octagonal, two are circular and the fourth is quadrilobed with small triangular spurs between the lobes. The church was dedicated in 1233 and Alexander II's wife Marie de Courcy was buried in the choir in 1241. Excavations showed it had a fully aisled nave ten bays long, transepts each with two east chapels and crossing piers study enough for a central tower, and a fully aisled presbytery three bays long with the eastern arcade piers as massive as those at the crossing. The bold diagonal corner buttresses added to the clasping pilasters of the north transept must have been later additions to a crossing and east end of c1170-1200, whilst the nave, with proper buttresses instead of pilasters, was probably added in the early 13th century.

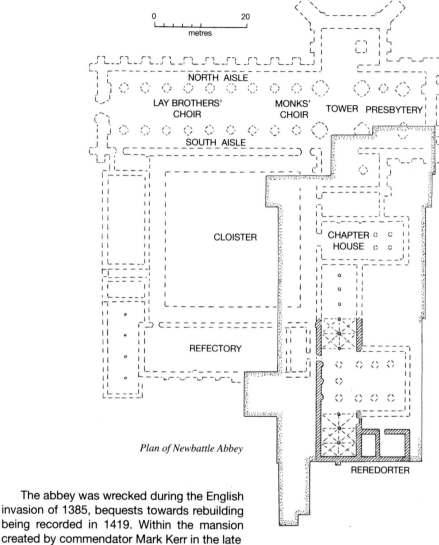

NORTH AISLE

LAY BROTHERS'
CHOIR

MONKS'
CHOIR

TOWER PRESBYTERY

SOUTH AISLE

CLOISTER

CHAPTER
HOUSE

REFECTORY

Plan of Newbattle Abbey

REREDORTER

The abbey was wrecked during the English invasion of 1385, bequests towards rebuilding being recorded in 1419. Within the mansion created by commendator Mark Kerr in the late 16th century are remains of the vaulted lowest storey of of the east range as then rebuilt. Three bays remain complete at the south end, where the reredorter projected to the east. This part was made a chapel in Victorian times and contains a font brought from Mavisbank house which bears the arms of James V, both his queen consorts, Ramsay of Dalhousie and James Haswell, abbot of Newbattle from 1529. North of this room are four bays of later work, and then two more medieval bays out of what were originally six extending north to where the chapter house projected. That room was divided by piers into three bays by two and was entered through a vestibule of three bays by two in the main range. A sacristy lay between it and the church. The refectory in the south range was aligned east-west and had the warming house at its east end.

NORTH BERWICK PRIORY   Lothian   *Cistercian Nuns*   NT 546850   West of town

In the grounds of a retirement home in Old Abbey Road lies a ruined mansion created c1587-90 by Alexander Home from the northern range of a nunnery founded c1150 with the Earl of Fife as patron. Originally Benedictine, it seems to have become Cistercian later on. There were still 21 nuns and a prioress here as late as 1544. The garden to the south represents the cloister and the church must have been to the south of that. The surviving range is late medieval and originally contained the refectory set over four vaulted cellars and a kitchen to the east. The Homes added the tower with a corbelled staircase turret on the north side beside the wall between the two rooms.

ORONSAY PRIORY   Argyll   *Augustinian*   NR 349889   Island to south of Colonsay

Both St Columba and St Oran are said to have been linked to a 6th century monastery here. The oldest parts of the existing ruin were under construction c1315-20 with John Macdonald, first Lord of the Isles as patron. Of that period are the east and north ranges set around a tiny cloister just 13m square with all four walks still surviving, with crudely made arcades on the south and west sides. The latter is a modern reconstruction of seven triangular-headed arches reusing two 16th century piers bearing black-letter inscriptions referring to an Irish craftsman named Mael-Sechlainn O'Quin working under the direction of Canon Celestinus.

The east range contained a dormitory over a warming house and a chapter house, the latter subdivided in the 18th century to create a burial aisle of the McNeils of Colonsay. A further extension was added east of here in the 19th century. The dormitory north gable collapsed in 1883. Although in later years the north range seems to have contained a refectory set over a kitchen, it may originally have formed the nave of the priory church. A lintelled doorway set within a wider arch leads through to an eastern compartment inclined to the south. Originally this room (now called the prior's chapel) could have formed the choir of the church. The west end of it has evidence of a former gallery or rood-loft. The east end, rebuilt in the 16th century, has one slit window on each side, another facing east, a platform for an altar and a fragment of a piscina.

North of this chapel lies a detached chamber called the prior's house. It lacks any fireplaces and may have once formed the reredorter. In 1927 this building was re-roofed to house a collection of cross fragments and twenty grave-slabs carved with motifs such as swords, animals, plants and galleys, plus ten low-relief human effigies including those of Canon Bricius MacMhuirich and Sir Donald MacDuffie, lay prior here in the 1550s. Another slab has an inscription referring to Murchardus Macduffie, d1539 with stags and hounds around a claymore hilt. To the east is a cross with a head of c1500-25 reset on a fragment of an earlier shaft..

A new church was provided along the south side of the cloister in the late 14th to early 15th century. It is a single chamber 18m long with upper and lower windows suggesting a former wooden gallery at the west end. Of c1500 is the lower part of what is assumed to be an intended west tower, beyond which is a fine cross with a Latin inscription referring to Colinus, son of Cristinus MacDuffie. The sculptor O'Quin (see above) is also named again. An added chapel forming the burial place of that family and have a tomb recess on the north side adjoins the south wall further east, leaving space for just one slit window between it and the SE corner buttress, within which is a L-shaped aumbry. On the north side an arch leads into a shallow space formed within the east range, probably for a sacristy. The late 15th century altar still remains and there is a three-light east window with intersecting tracery.

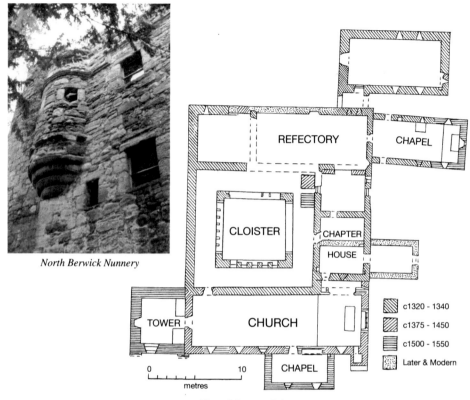

North Berwick Nunnery

REFECTORY

CHAPEL

CLOISTER

CHAPTER
HOUSE

TOWER

CHURCH

CHAPEL

0   10
metres

	c1320 - 1340
	c1375 - 1450
	c1500 - 1550
	Later & Modern

Plan of Oronsay Priory

Oronsay Priory from the SW

PAISLEY ABBEY   Renfrewshire   *Cluniac*   NS 486640   At east end of the town

Walter FitzAlan, High Steward of Scotland, founded this monastery in 1163, the original monks coming up from Wenlock in Shropshire, where the FitzAlans also had considerable estates. It originally ranked as a priory as was the norm for Cluniac houses, but visitation from so far away must have proved difficult and the house was upgraded to an abbey in 1245. In 1334 its head was further raised to the dignity of a mitred abbot. The abbey was jointly dedicated to St Mary, St James of Compostella, St Milburga (a saint associated with Shropshire) and the local Scottish saint St Mirin, to whom there is a vaulted chapel beside the south transept. This chapel was created in 1499 under patronage of James Crawford and became the burial place of the Hamiltons, one of whom was the last abbot. On the chapel east wall is an older frieze which is thought to depict scenes from the life of St Mirin, said to have come over from Ireland c560.

In the middle of the choir lies a tomb made up of fragments of other monuments and with an effigy of an abbot now on top. This was originally the tomb of Robert Bruce's daughter Marjory who married Walter, 6th High Steward. She was the mother of Robert II, first of the Stewart kings of Scotland, who is said to have been delivered by Caesarean section by monks at the abbey after the princess was mortally injured after falling from her horse. The tomb formed the centrepiece of a very long new 14th century choir of six aisleless bays which formed part of the rebuilding of the abbey after it was damaged by the English in the Wars of Independence. The fine ashlar-faced drain which runs under the buildings to the south formed part of the rebuilding. All that remains of the choir are the lower parts of the internal walls, including a set of four fine but rather damaged sedilia. The rest of what now stands, including a nine-light east window, dates from the restoration of 1912-28. The choir and transepts had been in ruins since the early 16th century when the central tower collapsed as a result of being weakened by a fire in 1498, although the transepts had survived in a more complete state.

The west doorway of Paisley Abbey   *The north arcade of Paisley Abbey*

The aisled nave with arcades of clustered piers is also of six bays but is rather shorter than the choir. Most of it dates from the 15th century, being completed by Abbot Thomas Tervas (1445-59). However the south aisle outer wall with a doorway with waterleaf capitals at the east end is of c1200, and of the 13th century are the lower parts of the west end with a very fine west doorway and an octagonal NW turret, plus the north doorway adorned with dogtooth and leaf capitals. Over the west doorway are a pair of three-light windows with cusped intersecting tracery and above them is a window with Flamboyant style tracery of c1500. The nave has a triforium of pairs of cinquefoiled cusped openings under moulded round arches, and then a clerestory with the very unusual feature of projecting brackets with large corbels set above each arcade pier to carry a gallery round from one window embrasure to the next instead of the jambs of the embrasures being pierced by a passage as was normal. The lowest corbel of each bracket is an animal head. The roof dates only from 1982. A tablet in the porch records a burial here of Abbot John Lithgow, d1433.

The building south of St Mirin's chapel takes the place of the chapter house but cannot be older than the 16th century since its west end blocks where the east alley of the cloister would be. The section of alley north of here, and the whole of the north alley beside the church have been rebuilt as a First World War memorial. Nothing remains of a west range but the south range containing the refectory still survives, although in a very much altered state.

Paisley Abbey

Doorway at Paisley Abbey

Trinitarian Friary at Crosskirk, Peebles from the NW, showing traces of a vaulted room in the west range

PEEBLES FRIARY   Borders   *Trinitarian*   NT 250407   North side of town centre

The discovery in the mid 13th century of what was later believed to be a relic of the true cross supposedly brought here in early times led to the construction of a substantial church 33m long by 10m wide externally, with a small sacristy on the north side. It may originally have been collegiate but by the 1440s was served by Trinitarian friars from the friary at Berwick, who later transferred their residence here. Only fragments of footings now remain of the full set of three domestic ranges that they added in the 1470s around a cloister 20m square on the north side, the sacristy becoming the southernmost room of the east range. There are traces of a vault over the southern-most room of the west range. At the reformation in 1560 the church was taken over by the parish since the parochial church of St Andrew further west had been burned by an English force in 1548. It remained in use until a new church was built in the High Street in 1784, although a new east wall was erected in 1656 to cut off the choir, which was then abandoned and is now reduced to the base of the walls. One original window was reset in the upper part of this new wall, dated 1656 on a lintel.

Most of the nave survives except that the western part of the nave south wall col-lapsed in 1811. This side seems to have had windows with tracery. West of the exist-ing east wall are traces of the bases of two nave altars against the rood screen. There seems to have been an arch here in the wall where the holy cross relic was displayed but rebuilding has removed the evidence. The Erskine burial aisle of c1804 now adjoins here, and on the north side is a burial aisle of c1705 of the Douglas earls of March. An original 13th century west doorway with water-holding bases and bell capitals now looks into a tower probably of the 1470s. It contained habitable upper rooms in some of the four storeys over a barrel-vaulted porch but the top is now fragmentary.

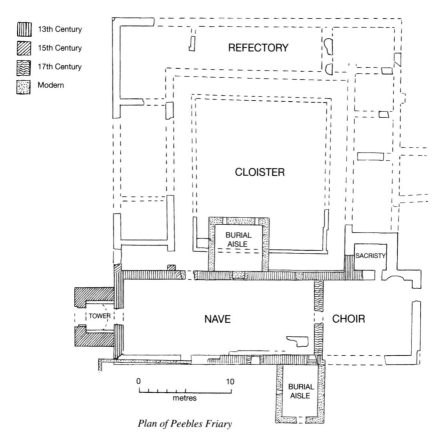

13th Century

15th Century

17th Century

Modern

REFECTORY

CLOISTER

BURIAL
AISLE

SACRISTY

TOWER

NAVE

CHOIR

0   10
metres

BURIAL
AISLE

Plan of Peebles Friary

PERTH FRIARY Perthshire *Carmelite* NO 108238 500m west of the city centre

This was the first Scottish house of the Carmelites, who were given a pre-existing chapel here by Richard, Bishop of Dunkeld in 1262. Building work here was in progress c1514. The site lay near Whitefriars Street, Longcauseway and Dovecot Land. Excavations of the footings of the 8m wide choir east end and the eastern range uncovered 21 burials, sherds of 13th century pottery and the matrix of the official seal of the friary.

PERTH FRIARY Perthshire *Dominican* NO 118239 North side of the city centre

Alexander II welcomed the Dominicans to Perth in 1231, establishing them in what is now Blackfriars Street just outside the northern defences, close to the site of the abandoned royal castle since the there was no vacant land available within the town centre. Kings and their consorts often stayed in the guest apartments and the friary was the favourite residence of James I. Here in 1437 he was murdered by Sir Robert Graham and others, despite the efforts of Catherine Douglas to use her arm as a bar to secure the door of the royal chamber. All the friaries in Perth were wrecked and suppressed in 1559 by Protestant Reformers following an inflammatory sermon preached in by John Knox in St John's church. Excavations near the Presto supermarket in 1983 revealed ditches of the Roman and Jacobite periods but no trace of the friary.

PERTH FRIARY Perthshire *Franciscan* NO 119233   SE corner of the city centre
The site beside Canal Street of the friary of Observant Franciscans, founded in 1460 by Lord Oliphant and wrecked and suppressed in 1559, has been a burial ground since James VI granted it to the town in 1580.

PERTH PRIORY Perthshire *Augustinian Nuns* NO 112229   SW of the city centre
Little is known about this house dedicated to St Leonard, except that by 1434 the nearby Carthusian priory had control over it and the nunnery was closed in 1438, although the chapel remained in use until c1560. The prioress was amongst the land-holders who were required to swear fealty to Edward I of England in 1296. In the days of steam trains an engine shed stood on the site, which is just to the south of Perth railway station.

PERTH PRIORY Perthshire *Carthusian*   NO 116234   Middle of the city centre
After his murder in the Dominican friary in 1437 James I was buried in the church of this friary which he had founded in 1429, probably intending it as his mausoleum. His English wife Joan Beaufort and James IV's English wife Margaret Tudor were also laid to rest here. Known as Domus Vallis Virtutis (House of the Valley of Virtue), it was the only charterhouse or priory of Carthusian monks that ever existed in Scotland, although Archibald, 4th Earl of Douglas had previously tried to set up such a house on his lands in 1419. The king spent on building the priory (under the supervision of a Cistercian monk called John of Bute) much of his own revenues and part of the funds which were supposed to pay his ransom due to England. He also persuaded other magnates and religious houses to reluctantly hand over lands and privileges to it, although some of them later tried to get their gifts back. By 1434 the priory had control of the hospital of St Mary Magdalene and the Augustinian nunnery of St Leonard both in the locality, the latter being closed a few years later.

Originally Carthusian charter-houses were supposed to ideally have a prior and twelve monks, following the example of Jesus Christ and the twelve apostles, but many of them were bigger than that. The accommodation at the fairly well preserved Carthusian priory at Mount Grace in Yorkshire indicates it always had rather more monks than thirteen. In 1478 the priory at Perth had a prior, fourteen monks, two lay brothers and one novice. Apart from attending church services the monks mostly studied and laboured alone, staying in their individual cells usually consisting of two or three rooms with a roofed but open sided passage leading past a garden to a lavatory set beside or within the outside boundary wall. This arrangement is still well-preserved at Mount Grace where one of the cells has been re-roofed and its garden re-planted. The monks mostly ate alone, being silently provided by the lay brothers with meals through L-shaped hatches, carefully arranged so that each monk could never see the person delivering his food. Only occasionally did they eat together in a refectory.

In May 1559 a band of reformers broke into the priory, wrecked it and killed one of the monks. Four monks then fled abroad, and Prior Adam Forman and another monk also went abroad in 1567, leaving just four monks at Perth, one of whom, Adam Stewart, was an illegitimate son of James V and took the title of prior. His nephew James VI granted the buildings and gardens to the townsfolk in 1569, but a few monks may have remained here until being ejected in 1600, following a re-issuing of the royal charter of 1569. The King James VI Hospital mostly of 1750, latterly private housing, lies on the site and may incorporate minor remains of the priory, or material reused from it.

The gatehouse of Pittenweem Priory

PITTENWEEM PRIORY   Fife

Augustinian NO 549025 E end of village

In the early 14th century the monastic community on the Isle of May transferred here, taking over an earlier church of which part of a doorway of c1200 still remains at the east end of the north side, its position indicating the building was once much longer. The arch on the south may also be medieval but the other features appear to be mid to late 16th century and 19th century, whilst the west tower of 1588 acts as the town tolbooth. Of 15th century monastic buildings to the south there remain a substantial east gatehouse with corbelling for a parapet and a west range which may have originally contained a dormitory over a refectory. This part was remodelled in the 1580s as the manse and is now known as Great House. This range also has a pend, and higher up are oriel windows on each of the east and west sides. See photo on page 21.

Pluscarden Priory from the SE

PLUSCARDEN PRIORY   Moray *Valliscaulian*   NJ 142577   8km SW of Elgin

Founded in 1230 by Alexander II, this was one of three daughter houses of Vallis Caulium in France that were established in Scotland at about the same time. It was dedicated to St Mary, St Andrew and St John the Baptist. Supposedly still visible on the internal walls of the church are marks of the burning it suffered in 1390 at the hands of Robert II's son Alexander Stewart, Earl of Mar, the notorious Wolf of Badenoch. In 1454 the Pope agreed to the impoverished priory being unified with that of the unreformed Benedictine priory of Urquhart to the east of Elgin. Prior John Bonally and one other monk from Urquhart transferred to Pluscarden, where three of the original monks stayed on, and three others went off to join the Cistercians at Kinloss and Deer.

James IV came here in 1506 as the guest of Prior Robert Harrower and "gave drink-silver to the masons working on the priory". Reset on the transept is a stone with the arms of the next prior, George Learmonth. By this era the Dunbar family controlled the priory lands as baillies. One of them, Alexander, was prior from 1529 to 1560 and was involved in the Dunbars' confrontation with the Innes family in the cathedral at Elgin in 1555. He added the vestry to the north side of the choir and the sacrament house backing onto it. At this time there is a record of the community having a chamberlain (another Dunbar) with two personal servants, plus a cook, baker, gate-porter and a gardener. It was later controlled by the Setons, who were Catholics and seem to have allowed the remaining monks to continue with Catholic forms of worship. The last monk, Thomas Ross, signed a charter along with Commendator Alexander Seton in 1587.

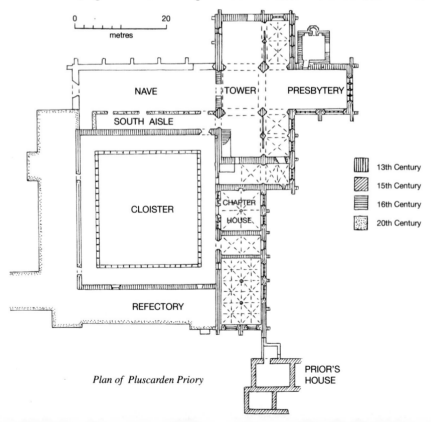

Plan of Pluscarden Priory

The priory passed through various hands until purchased in 1897 by John Patrick, 3rd Marquess of Bute, a Catholic convert. His son made three attempts to re-establish a religious community in the buildings before the Benedictines at Prinknash Abbey in Gloucestershire sent up five monks in 1948 to establish a community now numbering more than twenty, and since 1974 elevated to the status of an abbey. The crossing and eastern parts of the church and the eastern claustral range are now re-roofed and back in use and new south and west ranges have been built, the latter used for guests.

The mostly mid to late 13th century church currently consists of a low central tower with a parapet hardly rising above the roofs of transepts each with two vaulted east chapels, plus a choir three bays long. The crossing piers are quite badly defaced. The row of four sharply pointed lancets in the east wall and the three-light traceried window above are later medieval work set within an original frame. The vesica window in the gable is original. On the south side of the choir are two large three-light windows, now with restored tracery, whilst the transepts have tall lancets, mostly original. The position of the cloister (now with modern alleys) allows space for a narrow south aisle to the nave, a rare instance of a single aisle being placed on the side adjoining the cloister. The south aisle outer wall was completed high enough to abut a cloister alley against it and contains a finely moulded round-arched doorway. There is no certainty that the rest of the nave ever stood above the wall bases although the doorway is an indication of progress on this part. South of transept (in which are original night stairs) is a vaulted sacristy, east of which is what is now the Lady Chapel. Beside the sacristy is a square chapter house vaulted with a central pier. It has two-light windows on either side of the doorway and pairs of triple east lancets with the central one raised higher. The vaulted room of it was once a slype or passage, but the outer opening has been blocked. The south end of the range has a chamber with a pair of three-light east windows and two clustered piers supporting vaulting in three bays by two. The dormitory above has been much altered and restored and there is now also an attic in the roof.

RENFREW PRIORY   Renfrewshire

Cluniac   Location Unknown

In 1163 Cluniac monks arrived from Wenlock in priory to take possession of a priory here which was dedicated to St Mary and St James. The priory was soon abandoned and its pos-sessioned passed to the abbey at Paisley.

Night stair at Pluscarden   *Doorway from church to cloister at Pluscarden*

RESTENNETH PRIORY   Angus *Augustinian*   NO 482516   2km E of Forfar

The central tower of the church is built over an early porch which may go back to the early 8th century when St Boniface was sent up here from the monastery at Wearmouth with other monks at the invitation of Nechtan MacDerile, High King of the Picts. The mission specifically included masons for the construction of a church dedicated to St Peter. The tower itself must have existed by the end of the reign of Alexander I (1107-24), when the king built a palace at Invergowrie and had the annals of Iona transferred to Restenneth, probably because Iona lay amongst the islands ceded by Alexander's elder brother Edgar to the kingdom of Norway. Probably during David I's reign Augustinian canons replaced Celtic priests, and under a charter granted c1160 by Malcolm IV the priory was made subordinate to the abbey at Jedburgh.

The choir or chancel was probably completed just before August 1243 when the church was consecrated by David de Burnham, Bishop of St Andrews. The priory was burned during the Wars of Independence, losing its own charters and some others sent up from Jedburgh. Edward I of England in 1305 allowed the canons to have twenty oaks from a nearby royal forest for repairs, and in 1317 King Robert made a similar grant. He was a generous benefactor and his young son John was buried in the church.

The priory survived an attempt by James IV to suppress it and have its revenues annexed to the Chapel Royal of Stirling Castle. There had once been eight canons but by 1501 there were only two. The church served the parish of Forfar until 1591, after which a former chapel-of-ease in the town was developed as the parish church. Because of its connection with Jedburgh the priory was taken over by the Home family in the 1560s but in 1606 it went to the Earl of Kellie, later passing through several families, before officially becoming a state monument in 1919.

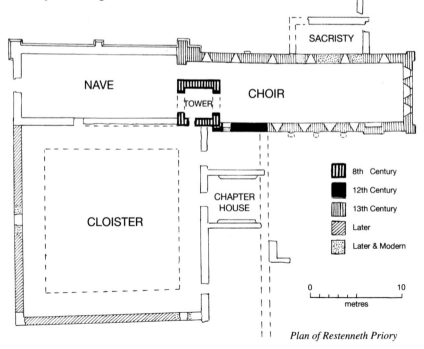

Plan of Restenneth Priory

A high wall of uncertain date surrounds the west and south sides of the cloister. Both the doorways in it are modern but the corbels for the cloister roof seem original, if at a higher level than normal. Of the east range there remain footings of the west wall against the cloister and of the north and south walls of a room identifiable as the chapter house from the benches built against both sides. The room north of it must have been a sacristy and part of the choir wall at that point, with a blocked doorway from the dormitory and a roof raggle for the lost range, is 12th century.

Overall the church is more complete although its nave along the north side of the cloister is reduced to foundations. The heavy northern buttresses probably dated from the same period as the choir, ie c1220-40. The choir has clasping east corner buttresses, three east lancets now lacking their heads, four lancets with trefoil-headed rere-arches and a sedilia recess and a piscina on the south side. The tomb recess further west on this side is later medieval. There are six lancets on the north, although the second and third lancets on that side lie in a section of wall rebuilt in modern times. Footings remain of a sacristy at this point. The tower is located so that there was room for a passage between the nave and choir to the north of it. Its north wall is solid and the south wall has an original doorway with a raised margin. The west arch must be an insertion of the 12th century when the nave was added. The east arch is original, or at least pre-12th century. The upper parts are 11th or very early 12th century work, with small triangular-headed belfry windows, but the broach spire is 15th century. Fixed to the inside of the tower north wall is an incised slab of one of the canons.

Two views of Restenneth Priory

ROXBURGH FRIARY Borders *Franciscans* NT 720337 To the SW of Kelso

The flat ground almost enclosed by the rivers Tweed and Teviot, and lying between the town of Kelso and the ridge bearing the ruins of the castle of Roxburgh, was once occupied by a flourishing walled town which was gradually abandoned during the 16th century. The Franciscan friary seems to have stood on the south side, near a gate in the wall and a bridge over the Tweed.

SADDELL ABBEY Argyll *Cistercians* NR 784321 On east side of Kintyre

This small Cistercian abbey was founded either by Somerled, Lord of Kintyre, killed in 1164 at Renfrew by Malcolm IV, or his son Reginald. The monks seem to have come from Mellifont in Co Louth in Ireland and remained subject to occasional visitation by the abbot of that house. In early 16th century the impoverished community was dissolved and its possessions added to those of the bishopric of Argyll then held by David Hamilton. He then immediately built the fine tower house now maintained by the Landmark Trust which lies on the shore east of the abbey. The graveyard contains rough low walls later partly rebuilt and used as parts of burial enclosures, but originally forming the undercroft of the refectory set east-west on the south side of the cloister and parts of the presbytery and north transept of the abbey church. Once about 41m long (according to the Statistical Account of 1794) the church was aisleless and there is no certain evidence that the transepts ever had eastern chapels. No details remain apart from a single piece of late 12th century moulding with chevrons and a roll in the presbytery. Rather more impressive is the collection (now gathered together in a display shelter) of 14th to 16th century grave-slabs depicting in low relief effigies of clerics, men in suits of chain mail, a huntsman, ships, swords and both mythical and real animals. Two pieces of a former free-standing 15th century cross also remain.

Half relief military effigies at Saddell

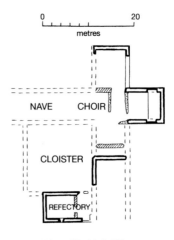

0 —————————— 20
metres

NAVE   CHOIR

CLOISTER

REFECTORY

Plan of Saddell Abbey

ST ANDREWS CATHEDRAL Fife *Augustinian*   NO 515167   East of the city

A shrine of St Andrew probably stood here in the mid 8th century. In 908 what was then Scotland's only bishopric was transferred here from Abernethy. Alexander I in 1124 got Robert, prior of the new Augustinian abbey at Scone, elected as bishop of St Andrews. It was Bishop Robert who installed Augustinian canons here to replace the Culdee priests, who then transferred to the church of St Mary of the Rock further east and seem to have survived there possibly as late as the 14th century. By 1147 the canons had gained the right to elect the bishops, and the church of St Regulus with its 33m high tower-nave had been newly built to serve them, and as a landmark for seafarers.

Arnold, formerly abbot of Kelso, became bishop in 1159 and soon began laying out foundations of what would then have been one of the longest churches in Britain to form a splendid new cathedral. Intended to be about 120m long externally, it was to have an aisled nave of fourteen bays, and a central tower with transepts long enough for each to have an aisle of three east chapels beyond the aisles of the choir. Of the eastern parts completed by c1200 there remain just the south and east walls of the south transept with a spiral staircase in angle between them, a few pier bases of the arcades, and the aisleless east end of the presbytery with spired octagonal turrets above angle buttresses and a large 15th century window above a row of three late 12th century round-headed windows of equal height. Wall passages mark the levels of the triforium and clerestory and there are traces of a 15th century high vault.

Plan of Arbroath Abbey

Of the nave there remains the outer wall of the south aisle with round arched windows of c1200 towards the east and pointed-headed windows of the 1270s with Y-tracery further west. These must be part of the work of Bishop Wishart, during whose time the west front partly collapsed in a gale. Just the southern half with one tall polygonal turret now remains of a new west front then built further east, thus shortening the nave by two bays. It must have been completed in time for the consecration by Bishop Lamberton in 1318, the ceremony being attended by King Robert, seven bishops, fifteen abbots and many nobles. It was Lamberton who had crowned King Robert at Scone in 1306 and had consequently suffered two years imprisonment in Winchester Castle by order of Edward I of England. Some of the piers in the transepts and nave were rebuilt after a fire in the 1370s, along with part of the central tower, but these parts with the coats of arms they once bore are now lost. This work was not completed until c1440 and the south transept gable required rebuilding after falling during a storm in 1409. St Andrews became an archbishopric in 1472. The townsfolk had their own parish church so the cathedral was not needed after the Reformation and was allowed to decay until the remnants became a state maintained monument as early as 1826.

South of the nave lay a cloister about 48m square, the largest in Scotland. Still remaining are the lower levels of the 13th century east and south ranges with piers supporting rib-vaults, and the 16th century barrel-vaulted southern half of the west range. A well on the south side marks the site of a lavatorium where the canons washed their hands before ascending to the lost refectory on the upper floor. South of the transept are remains of the chapter house with its entrance facade of a window on either side of a central doorway. This part became a vestibule to a larger new chapter house built further east in 1313-21, but now much ruined. At the south end of the east range are low walls of the reredorter and another building lies further east.

St Andrews has a large precinct still enclosed by a 0.9m thick 14th century wall with a main gatehouse on the west side and a later second gateway on the south. The upper parts of the 6m high wall and the many turrets furnished with gunloops are the work of Prior Patrick Hepburn, d1522.

West front of St Andrews Cathedral

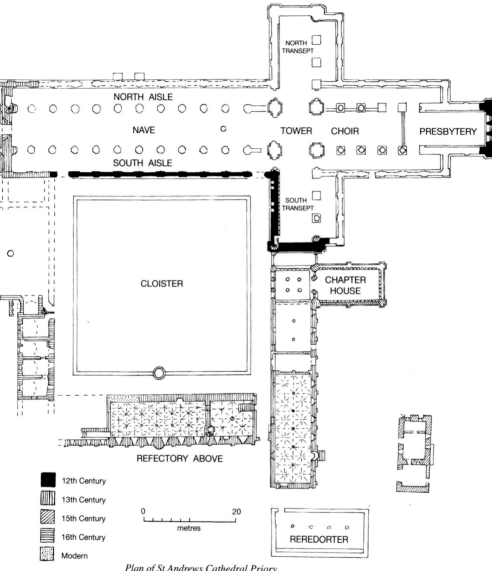

Plan of St Andrews Cathedral Priory

The bishops' dwelling at St Andrews took the form of a castle set on the next headland to the north of the precinct. Much of what remains is late 14th century work by Bishop Trail, but the Fore Tower goes back to the time of Bishop Roger c1200 and much of what faces the town was built c1550-70 by Archbishop John Hamilton. Mines still remain as relics of the long siege endured by a party of Protestants who took the castle was a strategem in 1546 and then murdered Cardinal David Hamilton within it. for more details see Castles of the Heartland of Scotland by Mike Salter, 2007.

The north transept of the Dominican friary church at St Andrews

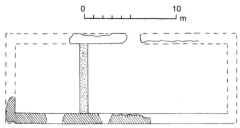

Plan of Strathfillan Priory Church

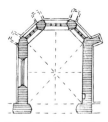

St Andrews Friary: plan

ST ANDREWS FRIARY Fife *Dominican* NO 506165 In the middle of the city

Madras College of 1832-4 stands on the site of the claustral buildings of a Dominican friary founded by Bishop Wishart in the 1270s. It was sacked by Protestant reformers in 1559. Of the church there survives the north transept encroaching upon the street, permission for building which was granted in 1525 by Archbishop Beaton. Rather unusually the transept has an apsed north end with the corners buttressed to take the weight of a ribbed tunnel vault, most of which still remains, with a boss with symbols of the Passion. One of the corbels supporting the ribs has the arms of the Hepburns, probably for John Hepburn, then prior of the Augustinian priory. On the east side is an aumbry with an ogival head. There are windows of three lights surmounted by a hoodmould with rosettes. That facing north has 19th century tracery imitating the intersecting tracery with a top circle of the NW window.

ST MARY'S PRIORY   Galloway *Augustinian*   On island 2km SW of Kirkcudbright

Fergus, Lord of Galloway is assumed to have founded this priory before 1161. William, Prior of Galloway is mentioned along with officials of Holyrood Abbey (the mother house) inn 1173, although the priory itself is first mentioned c1189-93. After the community dwindled James IV gave the lands back to Holyrood, whose prior then installed a secular kinsman to take charge at St Mary's. The exact location of the priory on the former island, now a peninsular jutting out into Kirkcudbright Bay, is uncertain. A font of the 1480s from here now lies in the garden of the Selkirk Arms Hotel, Kircudbright.

ST MONANS FRIARY   Fife *Dominicans*   NO 523014   To the SW of the village.

David II had this cliff-top church built in 1362-70, presumably intending it to serve a college. It is T-shaped rather than cruciform as it does not appear that a nave was ever even begun and consists of a tower with transepts and a choir extending eastwards for four bays. The rib-vault with heraldic bosses over the choir and perhaps the choir windows, date from after James III gave the church to the Dominicans in 1471. The choir was closed off from the rest as a parish church from 1647 to 1826. See plan and photo in the companion volume, Medieval Churches of Scotland

ST SERF'S PRIORY   Perth & Kinross *Augustinian*   NO 161002   5km SE of Kinross

A Culdee community said to have been established in 838 near the north end of an island in Loch Leven was replaced in 1145 by a few Augustinian canons from St Andrews. From that time survive the nave of a small church which in the 1830s was converted into a cottage. The chancel was demolished c1560, although its chancel arch remains and its wall footings have been revealed by excavations, which also uncovered remains of the canons' T-plan domestic building 200m to the west. A blocked 2m wide Norman arch in the nave west wall suggests that a west tower was intended.

SCONE ABBEY   Perth & Kinross *Augustinian*   NO 117265   3km north of Perth

Scone was a major monastic site from an early period and here in 838 Kenneth MacAlpine set up the Stone of Destiny taken from Dunstaffnage in Argyll. Here all the kings of Scotland were crowned up until the time of Charles II's coronation in 1651, even though Edward I of England had had the stone removed to Westminster Abbey in 1296 (it was returned to Scotland only in 1996) and the abbey at Scone had been destroyed by Protestant reformers in 1559. The crowning of Robert Bruce as King of Scotland here in 1306 resulted in the Bishop of St Andrews being imprisoned by Edward I in an English royal castle. Alexander I had six Augustinian canons sent here c1120 from Nostell in Yorkshire to establish a priory to replace the Culdees of the Celtic monastery, and it was upgraded to an abbey in 1164, being dedicated to the Holy Trinity and saints Augustine, Laurence, Mary and Michael. Part of the church seems to have remained in use as a parish church until some of it collapsed in 1624. A burial ground marks the site. Recent investigations have shown it was 70m long. A vaulted room to the south was discovered in 1841. The palace to the west is an early 19th century rebuilding of a late 16th and early 17th century mansion built after the lands were made into a temporal lordship for the Earl of Gowrie.

The canons of Scone maintained a chapel on an island at the west end of Loch Tay which is said to have been the burial place in the 1120s of Queen Sybilla, but there is no real evidence it was a separate priory as such. The existing ruins there are of a house built c1500 by the Campbells which was captured by General Monk in 1654.

SCOTLANDWELL FRIARY Perth & Kinross *Trinitarians* NO 186016 ESE of Kinross
Friar Place Burial Ground is the site of the hospital-friary of St Mary founded in 1210.

SOULSEAT ABBEY Galloway *Premonstratensians* NX 101587 5km ESE Stranraer
A rose garden at Inch Manse set on a promontory projecting into Soulseat Loch is said
to be the site of the cloister of the abbey founded c1152 by Fergus, Lord of Galloway
and which was described in 1386 as being ruined by wars. East of the manse are
traces of the base of a building about 21m long by 13m wide.

SOUTH QUEENSFERRY FRIARY Lothian *Carmelites* NT 129784 By Forth Br.
The Carmelites are said to have been established in this area by c1330, but the surviving church dates from after land was donated in 1441 by James Dundas of Dundas
for the construction of a church of St Mary and a set of claustral buildings. Nothing of
the latter remains except traces of the cloister roof on the north wall of the surviving
parts of the church, which comprise a central tower set on round arches opening into a
choir and south transept. The short ruined nave was removed c1875. Old plans show it
with a thin later west wall, suggesting a greater length was at least intended if not built.
The other parts were renovated in 1890 to form an Episcopal church, although the
ashlar tower (originally higher) remained in use as a dovecot until 1926. The choir has
a piscina, cusped-headed sedilia with basket arches, lancets and two-light windows
with minimal tracery. It is covered by a stone-slabbed roof over a pointed tunnel vault.
There is another vault under the tower, but the nave had a wooden roof. The choir east
wall has an image niche, blank shields and corbels for a belfry. The south transept has
a square-headed south window of three lights with cusped ogival heads.

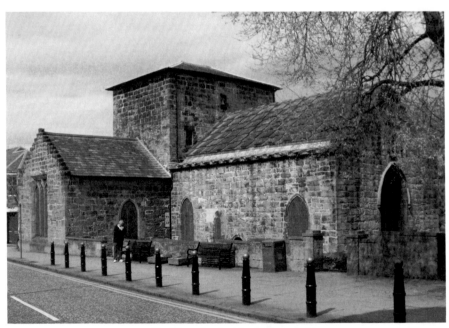

The friary church at South Queensferry

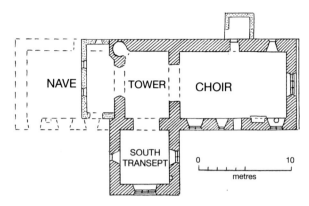

Plan of South Queensferry Friary Church

STIRLING FRIARY Stirlingshire   *Dominicans*   NS 796935   East side of old town

Excavations have revealed parts of the south and east walls of the church between Friars Street and the railway station.

STIRLING FRIARY Stirlingshire   *Franciscans*   NS 794935   Middle of old town

The Stirling Highland Hotel stands on the site of a friary of Observant Franciscans founded in the mid 15th century by Mary of Gueldres, wife of James II.

STRATHFILLAN PRIORY Stirling   *Augustinian*   NN 360284   NW of Crianlarich

The very ruinous oblong church is probably 14th century. The only feature is the sill of a south facing window near the west end, and the east and north walls are much broken down. The church served a daughter house of Inchaffray Abbey. See plan, page 126.

Last remains of the church of Strathfillan Priory

SWEETHEART ABBEY   Galloway *Cistercian*   NX 965662   10km S of Dunfries

Here in 1289 was buried Devorgilla, founder of this abbey for Cistercian monks back in 1273. The name Sweetheart refers to the ivory and silver casket buried with her, in which was kept the embalmed heart of her beloved husband John Balliol, lord of a great estate in northern England. In 1307 the abbot petitioned the elderly Edward I of England for compensation for £400 worth of damage caused by Welsh soldiers during his recent campaign in Scotland. In the 1380s the church was repaired after storm damage at the expense of Archibald, 3rd Earl of Douglas, Lord of Galloway. The Douglas arms also appear on what remains of the west range. In the 16th century the Maxwells became the protectors of the abbey lands and obtained some of them. Lord Maxwell refused to obey an order to destroy the abbey buildings issued in the 1560s.

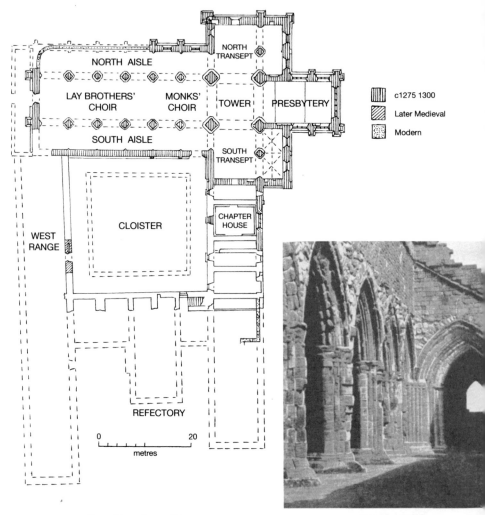

c1275 1300

Later Medieval

Modern

Plan of Sweetheart Abbey   *Sweetheart Abbey*

The last abbot or commendator was Gilbert Broun, who was exiled to France when the abbey was taken into royal hands in 1587. However he returned to the abbey, where he was arrested in 1603 and eventually deported after imprisonment at Blackness Castle. He was arrested again at Sweetheart in 1608 but allowed to remain under a form of house arrest. In 1609 his chamber was found to contain many artifacts considered to be "Popish trash". He appears to have died in retirement in Paris in 1612 and the abbey passed to the Spottiswode family, although in the 1630s it was briefly held by the newly created Bishop of Edinburgh.

South transept at Sweetheart Abbey

Of the claustral buildings a short section of wall between the cloister and west range and the east wall of the sacristy next to the south transept are the only original standing portions. Low walls remain of the northern part of the east range with wall-benches indicating the chapter house, and of the walls around the west and south sides of the cloister. The third room southwards of the chapter house was a warming house with a fireplace. The south range is assumed to have contained a kitchen in the SW corner and the refectory extending southwards with a projection for a reader's pulpit in the west wall. East of it lay the day stair and another room. Vaulted rooms probably of mid 16th century date survived here until c1800. The refectory seems to have been used as the parish church of New Abbey until demolished in 1731. One window from it was set into a new church built against the nave south wall which lasted until 1877. The reredorter projected eastwards from the east range roughly in line with the south range. The west range contained a dormitory for the lay-brothers over their refectory and other rooms. Fragments also remain of the 3.7m high abbey precinct wall, which had gateways facing NW and SE. A wet ditch substituted for the wall on the south side.

The church stands fairly complete except for most of the outer wall of the north aisle and the SW corner of the south aisle, which have gone, along with the aisle vaults. The church had a six bay nave with the monks' choir in the eastern two bays, a central tower and transepts each with two east chapels and a presbytery three bays long with triple sedilia on the south side. The eastern two chapels on the south side have 14th century vaulting with heraldic bosses covering a monument made up in 1933 from fragments of a 16th century replacement of the tomb of the foundress, which lay in the centre of the presbytery. The tower has the gables of a 16th century saddleback roof within a parapet on grotesque and human mask corbels. It was accessed from a spiral stair in a turret on the north transept NW corner. The nave has no triforium and the westernmost clerestory windows are repairwork of the 1380s. Blocking of that period containing a central two-light window and flanking single lancets has replaced the original four large lights and tracery of the great west window, but the original twelve-light wheel in the head still remains. There is a good doorway below these features, and a finer one, formerly with nook-shafts, at the east end of the south aisle. The presbytery had large traceried three-light windows on each side and a five-light east window with Geometrical tracery under a row of seven graduated lancets under a semi-circular arch. In the apex was a circular window with quatrefoil tracery.

TEMPLE PRECEPTORY   Lothian   *Knights Templar*   NT 313587   8km S of Dalkeith

The fine ruined church with gabled buttresses, three-light windows with intersecting tracery and good moulded rere-arches and a segmental tomb niche on the north side is an enigma. It seems too fancy to have simply served a small and remote parish, yet some details suggest it is two generations later than the suppression in 1312 of the Knights Templar, whose chief Scottish preceptory lay here. The western third of the church was rebuilt in the 17th century re-using axe-dressed ashlar blocks which may have come from a 12th century tower possibly further west. This suggests that the eastern part was a chancel or choir added in the 1360s or 70s to an older nave of the Templar period which survived until after the Reformation.

TONGLAND ABBEY   Dumfries   *Premonstratensian*   NX 698539   See below

To the west of the disused church of 1813 located 2km north of Kirkcudbright lies the west end of an older church of 1723. In the north wall of this lies a reset round-arched doorway decorated with some dogtooth which is the last relic of an abbey of Premonstratensian canons which was founded here in 1218 by Alan, Lord of Galloway.

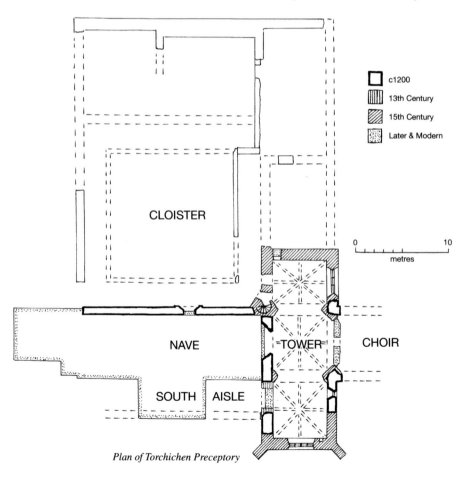

Plan of Torchichen Preceptory

TORPHICHEN   PRECEPTORY

Lothian   *Knights Hospitaller*
NS 969725   6km SW of Linlithgow

Torphichen was the headquarters of the Knights Hospitallers of St John of Jerusalem in Scotland and existed shortly before David I's confirmatory charter of 1153. The Hospitallers later became very wealthy, having acquired the former lands of the Templars after that order was suppressed in 1312. Their Scottish possessions included houses in Glasgow and Linlithgow. Preceptor Sir William Knollys was also keeper of the palace of Linlithgow for James IV and was made Lord St John. The last preceptor here was Sir James Sandilands, appointed in 1547. He joined the Reformation party and was made Lord Torphichen, having resigned the lands to the crown and getting them regranted to him as a temporal barony.

Torphichen Preceptory

More remains visible here than at any other Hospitaller preceptory in Britain. Only fragmentary foundations survive of a cloister north of the nave of the church and of ranges of buildings east and west of it. Fragments of bases and capitals of the cloister alley arcades lie elsewhere on the site. The lower courses of the late 12th century north wall with a blocked doorway of two orders survive of the nave, the site of which is now occupied by a T-plan parish church of 1756. A fine arch of c1180-1200, now blocked, opened into a central tower. Together with the transepts as rebuilt and given new windows and vaults in the 15th century (plus a 16th century saddleback roof on the tower) this part remains intact and still roofed, having continued in use as a court house after the Reformation. An inscription on the north transept vault refers to Sir Andrew Meldrum, preceptor in the 1430s. The south transept was extended slightly to the south when rebuilt and that end of it has diagonal corner buttresses and a tomb recess below a four-light window. An arch in the transept west wall led into an aisle four bays long added to the south side of the nave. Nothing remains of the late 12th century choir which may have been taken down early in the 16th century prior to a rebuilding which never happened. Against the west arch under the tower is a monument erected in 1538 by Preceptor Walter Lyndsay to his uncle and predecessor Sir George Dundas.

URQUHART PRIORY   Moray   *Benedictine*   NJ 294631   7.5km east of Elgin

David I founded a Benedictine priory here as a daughter of Dunfermline in 1125. By 1454 it was impoverished and had just a prior and one other monk, who transferred to Pluscarden in an amalgamation of the two houses. After the Reformation the priory went to Alexander Seton, later Earl of Dunfermline. Nothing now remains of it. The wheel-cross now in the church hall further south is an older Early Christian relic.

WHITHORN PRIORY   Galloway   *Premonstratensians*   NX 445404   W of village

St Ninian established a bishopric here in the early 5th century and erected a small stone church which became a shrine after he was canonised. The community serving the church became monastic by the 8th century but the bishopric was in abeyance until revived c1128 presumably at the instigation of Fergus, Lord of Galloway. He is thought to have brought in Augustinian canons to serve a small new cruciform cathedral church. In the 1170s the community seems to have adopted the stricter Premonstratensian rule. In the 13th century, when there were twenty canons in addition to the bishop and prior, the original nave was doubled in length and the transepts and choir rebuilt on a much larger scale, the new choir being six bays long with aisles flanking all except the east bay in which was St Ninian's shrine, thus creating a church 70m long.

By 1408 there were only twelve canons and the church was reported to be in a decayed state that was considered unseemly for such a major place of pilgrimage. This resulted in the Pope issuing an order that half of the priory's income was to be devoted to repairs. Princess Margaret, wife of the Earl of Douglas had a new chapel added in 1424 and c1430 Prior Thomas McGilliachnisy added a Lady Chapel extending south of the SE corner of the choir. James IV frequently came on pilgrimage to Whithorn and in 1491 and 1502 gave "drink-silver" to the masons employed on rebuilding works. As late as 1560 Bishop Alexander Gordon was given 500 merks from the royal treasury towards repair work on the cathedral church.

The church fell into decay after a 1581 Act of Parliament prohibited pilgrimages but at the beginning of the 17th century the nave was renovated for use as a parish church and a modest west tower then added. The other parts of the cathedral church were then all demolished and the only remains of them are a set of crypts lying under the east of the choir, the lady chapel to the south of it and the sacristy to the north. The choir crypt has heavily buttressed outer corners and now has two rooms with 15th century tunnel-vaults, but originally it was one chamber with vaults carried on a central pillar. East of this crypt low modern walls mark out what is thought to be the site of the 5th century church supposedly revealed by late 19th century excavations. A curious dome-vaulted chamber opens off the west side of the crypt below the former Lady Chapel. Of the claustral buildings to the north all that remains is part of the east range west wall incorporated in the present parish church of St Ninian built in 1822, with a slightly tower added to the north end.

The old nave remained in use until the church of 1822 was built, although the west end was walled off and galleries installed around three sides after the tower collapsed in the 1690s. Raising of the floor level in the 1630s has partly buried two 14th century tomb recess on the north side. The windows on the south side are 15th century, shortened to accommodate a lowered wall-head of the early 17th century. The round arched SE doorway cutting through a former tomb recess of c1200 is reset 15th century work from the choir or Lady Chapel and has a lion rampant under a crown on the hoodmould keystone and label stop angels bearing shields, one of which has the arms of Vaux. This local landed family supplied bishops Alexander (1422-50) and George (1482 to 1508), and Patrick, prior from 1478 to 1514. The SW doorway is an even more splendid piece put together in the early 17th century using stones with chevrons and other Romanesque motifs from a doorway and at least one internal arch remaining from the 12th century church. Walls of that era remain on either side of the eastern half of the nave, where there are small pilaster buttresses on the south side. The 17th century pulpit lay below a window of that period in the middle of the south wall.

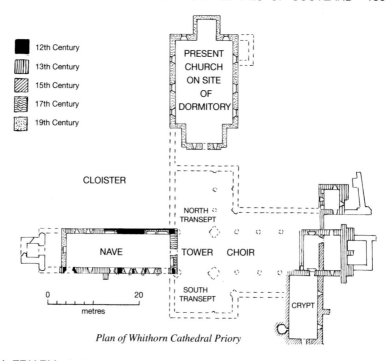

12th Century
13th Century
15th Century
17th Century
19th Century

PRESENT
CHURCH
ON SITE
OF
DORMITORY

CLOISTER

NORTH
TRANSEPT

NAVE   TOWER   CHOIR

0   20

metres

SOUTH
TRANSEPT

CRYPT

Plan of Whithorn Cathedral Priory

WIGTOWN FRIARY Galloway *Dominican* NX 436554 Below east side of town

This friary, dedicated to St Mary, seems to have been founded in 1267 with Devorguilla
Balliol as the main patron. It is last recorded in 1400 and may not have survived until
the Reformation. Some walls are said to have remained until the early 19th century. A
geophysical survey in 2003 found some ditches and minor footings of two buildings.

The nave of Whithorn Cathedral

GLOSSARY OF TERMS

Aisle	-	A passage beside part of a church.
Antae	-	Projections of north and south walls of a church beyond end gables.
Apse	-	A semi-circular chapel or a similarly shaped east end of a church.
Ashlar	-	Masonry of large blocks cut to even faces and square edges.
Aumbry	-	A recess for storing books or vessels.
Bays	-	Divisions of an elevation defined by regular vertical features.
Chancel	-	The eastern member of a church reserved for priests and choristers.
Chapter House	-	A room where monks, priests or friars met daily to conduct business.
Chevrons	-	Vs usually arranged in a continuous sequence to form a zigzag.
Choir	-	A part of a monastic church containing stalls for monks, nuns or friars.
Clerestory	-	An upper storey pierced by windows lighting the floor below.
Cloister Alley	-	A walkway along one side of a cloister.
Cloister Garth	-	The central court or garden of a cloister, surrounded by four alleys.
Commendator	-	One holding monastic revenues in trust when no abbot is appointed.
Corbel	-	A projecting or overhanging stone bracket.
Cruciform Church	-	Cross-shaped church with transepts forming the arms of the cross.
Cusps	-	Projecting points between the foils of a foiled Gothic arch.
Dado	-	Lower part of a wall, or its decorative treatment.
Dog-tooth	-	Four cornered stars placed diagonally and raised pyramidally.
Fleuron	-	Decorative carved shape like a flower or leaf.
Hood-moulding	-	A narrow band of stone projecting out over a window or doorway.
Jamb	-	The side of a window, doorway or other opening.
Lancet	-	A long and comparatively narrow window, usually pointed headed.
Lavatorium	-	A lavatory or washing place, usually next to the refectory entrance.
Mendicant	-	Begging, or living solely on alms.
Nave	-	The part of a church in which the lay congregation stood or sat.
Ogival Arch	-	Topped by a curve which is partly convex and partly concave.
Oratory	-	Small chapel either standing alone or forming part of a large building.
Oriel	-	A bay window projecting on corbelling.
Piscina	-	A stone basin used for rinsing out holy vessels after a mass.
Presbytery	-	The part of a monastic church containing the high altar.
Prior	-	The head person of a priory or friary or the deputy head of an abbey.
Pulpitum	-	Stone screen shutting off a choir, forming a backing for choir stalls
Quoin	-	A cut stone used to form part of a corner.
Refectory	-	The main dining room of a monastic house.
Rere-arch	-	An arch on the inside face of a window embrasure or doorway.
Reredorter	-	The toilet of a monastic house, usually at the far end of a dormitory.
Respond	-	Half pier bonded into a wall and carrying one end of an arch.
Reticulation	-	Window tracery with a net-like appearance.
Rood Screen	-	A screen with a crucifix mounted on it between a nave and a chancel.
Sacristy	-	A part of a church were vestments and sacred vessels were kept.
Sedilia	-	Seats for clergy (usually three in the south wall of a chancel or choir.
Spandrel	-	The surface between two arches or between an arch and a corner.
Transept	-	A cross-arm projecting at right-angles from the main body of a church
Transom	-	A horizontal member dividing upper and lower lights in a window.
Triforium	-	Middle storey of a church, either a blind arcade or an arcaded passag
Vesica	-	A pointed oval or eye-shaped opening.
Walking Place	-	A cross passage between the nave and the choir of a friary church.
Warming House	-	The only room in a monastery with a fireplace (apart from the kitchen)